Braids

Olivia Hannah

Cheer Up Slug

Tamsin Daisy Rees

T0027201

methuen | drama

LONDON • NEW YORK • OXFORD • NEW DELHI • SYDNEY

METHUEN DRAMA
Bloomsbury Publishing Plc
50 Bedford Square, London, WC1B 3DP, UK
1385 Broadway, New York, NY 10018, USA
29 Earlsfort Terrace, Dublin 2, Ireland

BLOOMSBURY, METHUEN DRAMA and the Methuen
Drama logo are trademarks of Bloomsbury Publishing Plc

First published in Great Britain 2021

Braids © Olivia Hannah, 2021

Cheer Up Slug © Tamsin Daisy Rees, 2021

Olivia Hannah and Tamsin Daisy Rees have asserted their right under
the Copyright, Designs and Patents Act, 1988, to be identified as the
Authors of these works.

Cover photo by Von Fox Promotions

A catalogue record for this book is available from the British Library.

A catalog record for this book is available from the Library of Congress.

ISBN: PB: 978-1-3502-9973-3
ePDF: 978-1-3502-9974-0
eBook: 978-1-3502-9975-7

Series: Modern Plays

Typeset by Mark Heslington Ltd, Scarborough, North Yorkshire
Printed and bound in Great Britain

To find out more about our authors and books visit
www.bloomsbury.com and sign up for our newsletters.

live
theatre

presents the world premiere of

Braids + Cheer Up Slug

A double bill of plays about young
women growing up in the North East

Braids by Olivia Hannah
Cheer Up Slug by Tamsin Daisy Rees

Thursday 7 – Saturday 23 October 2021

Braids

By Olivia Hannah

CAST

Xsara-Sheneille Pryce	Abeni
Rochelle Goldie	Jasmine

CREATIVE & PRODUCTION TEAM

Olivia Hannah	Writer
Kemi-Bo Jacobs	Director
Anna Orton	Designer
Drummond Orr	Lighting Designer
David Flynn	Sound Designer
Lou Duffy	Costume Supervisor
Craig Davidson	Stage Manager
Heather Robertson	Deputy Stage Manager

'Don't you ever get sick of it?'
'Being the only one?'
'Yeah. Being the Ambassador of Blackness?'

Abeni is new to college. She's putting purple braids in Jasmine's hair and giving her 'the talk', opening Jasmine's mind to new ways of seeing the world – and the world seeing both of them.

A new play by Olivia Hannah, about fitting in and standing out.

Long-listed for the Alfred Fagon Award 2018. Featured as part of BBC Arts Light Up Festival.

A word from writer Olivia Hannah:

'Braids *is a play about friendship, identity and belonging. And hair. It's inspired by my own experiences of growing up as a mixed-race girl in an English village, all wrapped up in a fictional story about a life-changing friendship, but it will feel familiar to anyone who has wondered where in the world they belong or how to move forward after life takes an unexpected turn.*'

CAST

Xsara-Sheneille Pryce   Abeni

Xsara-Sheneille Pryce is an actress of British Caribbean descent, born and raised in Birmingham. Since graduating from the Manchester School of Theatre in 2019, she has performed at The Royal Exchange and HOME theatre in Manchester and has had her TV debut on Sky Atlantic's *Tin Star* and the BBC.

These works include working with director Roy Alexander Weise on the production of *Luminosity*, alongside other shows in her final year such as *The Taming of the Shrew* and *The Last Days of Judas Iscariot*.

Passionate about history and black culture, she is also an aspiring writer particularly interested in telling stories of her cultural origin; stories handed down over generations that need to be told.

Rochelle Goldie   Jasmine

A proud northern actor who is lucky enough to train with top acting coaches in Los Angeles and represented by Wintersons.

This is Rochelle's second professional theatre job but her first taking a lead role on the stage. She is so grateful and excited to step out of her comfort zone and bring the character of Jasmine to life!

You will be able to catch Rochelle in *Vera* on ITV in 2022. Previous credits also include *A Series of Light* on Amazon Prime, *Waiting for Gateaux* (stage) and also the music video for Camden Town by Frikan which she took to the streets of London to star in and co-direct.

Olivia Hannah   Writer

Olivia Hannah is a Newcastle-based scriptwriter. *Braids* is her first full-length play. It was written as part of the Royal Court Writers' Group (North) in 2018 and long-listed for the Alfred Fagon Award. She is an Associate Artist at Live Theatre where *Braids* was first commissioned. In 2019, her short play *Michelle* was performed as part of Workie Ticket Theatre Company's *Women Warriors* project, working with female veterans to share their experiences. She is a recipient of a 2019 Slate R&D commission from Eclipse to develop an interactive theatre piece around Northern Soul and Black diaspora music in Newcastle in the 1970s. In 2020, her second full-length play *Shit Life Crisis* was long-listed for the Paines Plough Women's Prize for Playwriting and is currently being developed with Hull-based theatre company Silent Uproar. Olivia also writes film and TV, and a feature film version of *Braids* is currently in development.

Kemi-Bo Jacobs   Director

Kemi-Bo Jacobs trained as an actress at LAMDA. Her acting credits include Hermione in *The Winter's Tale* (RSC); Anne Deever in *All My Sons* (Manchester Royal Exchange) and Thea Elvsted in *Hedda Gabler* (Salisbury Playhouse). *Braids* is her directorial debut.

Cheer Up Slug

By Tamsin Daisy Rees

CAST

Jackie Edwards	Bean
David Fallon	Will

CREATIVE & PRODUCTION TEAM

Tamsin Daisy Rees	Writer
Anna Ryder	Director
Anna Orton	Designer
Drummond Orr	Lighting Designer
David Flynn	Sound Designer
Lou Duffy	Costume Supervisor
Craig Davidson	Stage Manager
Deputy Stage Manager	Heather Robertson

'Not that I'm saying I know more about you than you do, I'm not saying that, that's not what I'm saying, like, at all! Just that I do know you better than maybe you know yourself.'

Will and Bean have been friends forever. But they're not kids anymore and the adult world is a scary place. In a tent in County Durham, a Duke of Edinburgh Award trip becomes more complicated that either of them planned.

A new play by Live Theatre Associate Artist, Tamsin Daisy Rees about boundaries and behaviour.

A word from writer Tamsin Daisy Rees:

'Cheer Up Slug is a really special play for me. It was the first proper full length play I wrote, and has been on various journeys but has found it's home with Live Theatre. It's a funny, awkward, sad play about teenage relationships and understanding and not understanding the boundaries and care you deserve. I am so excited to be working with Anna – her vision, care and kindness towards this story is making it what it is.'

Cast

Jackie Edwards Bean

Jackie Edwards is a North East based actor, writer and facilitator. She started acting at Live Youth Theatre, for whom she is now a regular facilitator. Her acting credits include: *The Dumping Ground, Inside Out* (BBC); *My Mate Ren* (Sticky Theatre); *From The Ashes* (Curious Monkey) and numerous *10 Minutes To* productions (Live Theatre). She has also worked with Alphabetti, New Writing North, Circus Central and Tyneside Cinema.

She is a member of the comedy troupe Your Aunt Fanny: *Minge Unhinged* (debut tour, 2019); *Bonnie and Fanny's Christmas Spectacular* (Live Theatre, 2019); *Your Aunt Fanny's Cum Back* (Cumberland Arms, 2021). The group are currently producing a podcast, as well as their next full length show *Muff Said*.

Jackie is passionate about North East stories, and has produced and performed in a film of a folktale she wrote herself, *Some Said: The North Sea Beast*, and she is working towards producing her second.

David Fallon Will

David Fallon graduated from Rose Bruford College in 2019.

Theatre credits: *Scouts! The Musical* (BEAM Festival/Hackney Empire); *Baba Yaga* (Theatre Hullabaloo); *The Prince and The Pauper* (Watermill Theatre); *Hedda Tesman* (Workshop, Headlong/Chichester Festival Theatre); *Pardoned* (The Other Palace Studio.)

Credits whilst training: *Life, Apparently, City of Angels, Vernon God Little, Diary of a Scoundrel, A Midsummer Night's Dream, Middletown.*

Tamsin Daisy Rees   Writer

Tamsin is a playwright from County Durham, now based in Newcastle upon Tyne. She is a member of the Orange Tree Writer's Collective 2021, an Associate Artist at Live Theatre and was a member of the first Royal Court Writers' Group North. She writes stories that are rooted in the North East and prod at class, sexuality and power. Tamsin is also currently an AHRC-funded PhD candidate at Newcastle University where she is specialising in playwriting.

Previous theatre work includes: *Fledglings* (Nuffield Southampton Theatres); *Clementines* (Live Theatre); *My Mate Ren* (Sticky Theatre); *Teddy* (New Writing North); *Fingerwank* (Live/Bunker Theatre).

Anna Ryder   Director

Anna is a freelance theatre director specialising in developing new writing. She has predominantly directed work in the North East region and has worked with companies including the RSC, Paines Plough, Northern Stage, Royal Exchange Manchester, New Writing North and Mortal Fools. Anna is an Associate Artist of Live Theatre, Newcastle.

Directing credits: *Look, No Hands* (Pleasance, London and Pitlochry Festival Theatre); *Spring REVEL* (RSC); *Locker Room Talk* (Live Theatre); *Teddy* (Durham Book Festival); *Stupid* (Mortal Fools); *Melva* (Mortal Fools); *Get Yourself Together* (Royal Exchange); *Rendezvous* (Live Theatre).

Assisting and Associate credits: *The Whip* and *King John* (RSC); *Lands: Beating The Bounds* (Live Theatre); *Broken Biscuits* (Paines Plough); *Get Carter* (Northern Stage. JMK Regional Bursary recipient); *Wet House* (Live Theatre); *Tallest Tales from the Furthest Forest* (Northern Stage).

Anna Orton   Set & Costume Designer

Anna's previous designs include, *La Bohème* (Scottish Opera); *Cendrillon* (Buxton Opera Festival); *The Effect* (English Theatre Frankfurt); *A Christmas Carol* (Pitlochry Festival Theatre); *Messiah* (Bristol Old Vic Theatre/Bridgewater Hall Manchester/UK cinema release); *King Lear* (Bristol Old Vic Theatre Royal); *Extraordinary Wall of Silence* (Theatre Ad Infinitum /Bristol Old Vic Theatre/UK tour); *Philistines* (Jerwood Vanbrugh Theatre); *Trojan Women* (Bristol Old Vic Studio); *Arachnophilia* (Dublin Fringe Festival); *No Kids* (Theatre Ad Infinitum/UK/international tour) and *Champ* (Tobacco Factory, Bristol).

Anna has an MA Theatre Design (Bristol Old Vic Theatre School) and an MA Fine Art BA Hons, (Duncan of Jordanstone). www. annaorton.com

Drummond Orr   Lighting Designer

Drummond has over forty years' experience as a theatre electrician, technical manager, lighting designer and production manager. In that time, he has toured nationally and internationally, and has worked in both touring and production theatre.

Recent lighting design credits for Live Theatre include: *The Red Lion* (Live/Trafalgar Studios); *My Romantic History, The Savage, Cooking With Elvis* and *Wet House* (Live/Hull Truck/Soho Theatre); *Tyne, The Prize, Nativities, Two Pints* and *A Walk On Part* (Live/Soho Theatre/Arts Theatre); *Blackbird* (Market Theatre, Johannesburg) and *The Girl in the Yellow Dress* (Market Theatre, Johannesburg/ Grahamstown Festival/Baxter Theatre, Cape Town/Citizens, Glasgow). *Educating Rita* (Theatre by the Lake/David Pugh and UK tour).

David Flynn   Sound Designer

David trained in media production before working in theatre, events and live music as a sound engineer and AV technician. He is currently technical manager for Live Theatre, one of the UK's leading new writing theatres renowned for producing and presenting new plays. David is also a freelance sound designer. Sound Design credits include: *Educating Rita* (national tour, Theatre by the Lake/ David Pugh); *Clear White Light, My Romantic History*, Olivier Nominated *The Red Lion* (Live/Trafalgar Studio's London); *The Savage, Harriet Martineau Dreams of Dancing, Flying into Daylight, Wet House* (Live/Hull Truck/Soho Theatre); *Cooking with Elvis, Faith* and *Cold Reading, A Walk on Part* (Live/Soho Theatre/Arts Theatre London); *A Northern Odyssey.*

About Live Theatre

'*One of the most fertile crucibles of new writing*' **The Guardian**

Live Theatre is a leading force in the creation of new plays. It produces world class plays and discovers, nurtures and develops emerging theatre makers. It creates high quality, contemporary plays that are socially engaging, entertaining and steeped in the questions and issues of today. Live Theatre reflects the wide range of backgrounds and culture within the North East and champions work from this region. Live Theatre is the only theatre in England, outside London, dedicated to the production of new plays. It has been doing this for almost 50 years.

'*Live Theatre has supported generation after generation of new writers, actors and theatre artists.*' **Lee Hall Playwright**

For more information see www.live.org.uk

Live Theatre Staff

Executive Director/Joint Chief Executive	**Jacqui Kell**
Artistic Director/Joint Chief Executive	**Jack McNamara**
PA to Joint Chief Executives	**Clare Overton**

Creative Programme

Interim Executive Producer	**Graeme Thompson**
Projects Producer	**John Dawson**

Children and Young People

Children and Young People's Programme Leader	**Helen Green**
Senior Creative Associate Children and Young People	**Paul James**
Creative Lead Live Tales	**Ross Wylie**
Creative Associate CYPP	**Becky Morris**

Technical Production

Production Manager	**Drummond Orr**
Technical and Digital Manager	**David Flynn**
Technician	**Craig Spence**

Operations and Finance

Finance Manager	**Antony Robertson**
Finance Officer	**Catherine Moody**

Development

Director of Development and Enterprise	**Lucy Bird**

Marketing and Communications

Marketing and Communications Manager	**Lisa Campbell**
Marketing and Communications Manager	**Michele McCallion**
Marketing and Communications Officer	**Caitlin Ivory**

Customer Services and Box Office

Customer Services and Estate Manager	**Nichola Ivey**
Duty Manager	**Michael Davies**
Duty Manager	**Ben Young**
Duty Manager and Bar Supervisor	**Alicia Meehan**
Duty Manager and Bar Supervisor	**Arthur Roberts**
Bar Supervisor	**Patrycja Nowacka**
Customer Service Assistant	**Beth Clarke**
Customer Service Assistant	**Brennan Flanders**
Customer Service Assistant	**Cameron John Sharp**
Customer Service Assistant	**Fay Carrington**
Customer Service Assistant	**Kay Greyson**
Customer Service Assistant	**Lewis Grey**
Customer Service Assistant	**Max Easter**
Customer Service Assistant	**Patrycja Nowacka**
Customer Service Assistant	**Sarah Matthews**
Customer Service Assistant	**Steven Blackshaw**
Customer Service Assistant	**Zoe Lamming**
Box Office Assistant	**Jasper Wilding**

Housekeeping

Housekeeping
Housekeeping
Housekeeping

Angela Salem
Jean Rent
Lydia Igbinosa

Supported by
ARTS COUNCIL ENGLAND

Newcastle City Council

Braids

Olivia Hannah

Characters

Jasmine, *18, mixed race, born and brought up in County Durham.*

Abeni, *19/20, Black, dark-skinned, from South Manchester, a new arrival to the region.*

Locations

City of Durham

A village in County Durham

Notes

– indicates speech broken off or an abrupt change of direction.

. . . indicates hesitation, or speech trailing off.

/ indicates where the next line begins.

A question without a question mark is delivered in a flat tone.

Scene One

December 2017. **Jasmine** *and* **Abeni** *enter a hair shop.* **Abeni** *is interested,* **Jasmine** *is unsure. They stand and look up at where a huge selection of hair is displayed.* **Jasmine** *is even more overwhelmed.*

Jasmine   There's just . . . so many options . . .

Abeni   Anything you could want. (*Beat.*) So what do you want?

Jasmine   I don't know . . . just . . . hair. For braiding. Is this all for braiding?

Abeni   Well, no. Some of it's real hair, for weaves. You don't want that. You want the synthetic stuff.

Jasmine   OK . . .

Abeni   There's purple. You wanted purple, right?

Jasmine   Yeah . . .

Abeni   You don't sound sure.

Jasmine   No, I am. I do. I think? I don't know. What do you think?

Abeni   Not up to me, babe. You're the one who's gonna be walking around with it on your head. Say what you feel.

Jasmine   No, no, I wanted purple. Right?

Abeni   Yeah, but we can still get some regular black or brown hair, do something a bit more/

Jasmine   Boring.

Abeni   I was going to say natural.

Jasmine   Oh. Yeah. It's just, I wanted colour. (*Pause.*) But if you don't think I can pull it off . . .

Abeni   Nah nah nah. Don't do that. Like I said, *I* think you're gonna look peng. I'm just making sure you want it.

Jasmine I do! I do. (*Trying to be casual.*) I just think people are going to be surprised.

Abeni Hell yeah they will! I can just see you striding into college on Monday, and everyone at the smoking shelter turns to watch you go past, like 'who is that buff babe with the purple braids?'

Jasmine (*scared but exhilarated*) Oh. Wow. Yeah.

Pause.

Abeni Mum used to do my braids. She liked having me captive so she could give me the Mum Lectures. (*African Mum voice.*) Did you know, Jasmine, that in many parts of Africa braids are used as a kind of code?

Jasmine I did not know that, Abeni.

Abeni How you wear your braids says something about you. Where you're from, if you're married or on the market. Who your people are.

Jasmine That's actually quite cool.

Abeni Right? So maybe if we work out what you want to say, we'll know if bright purple braids are the best way to say it.

Jasmine I mean . . . I don't want to say anything. I just thought they looked cool.

Abeni No way. They spoke to you on a deeper level. We'll work it out.

Jasmine I don't think it's that deep. (*Beat.*) I'm so glad you moved up here.

Abeni Makes one of us.

Jasmine Really? Still.

Abeni No, not really. I mean, yeah, sometimes . . . it's fine. I feel a bit cut off. And I'm not used to being the only Black person in the room. It happens a lot here.

Jasmine   That's my normal. It was more surprising when I seen you.

Abeni   Don't you get sick of it?

Jasmine   Being the only one?

Abeni   Yeah. Being the Ambassador of Blackness.

Jasmine   Ambassador of Blackness?

Abeni   You know. Feeling like you can't ever mess up. Fielding questions about anything and everything to do with Black people. Any Black people.

Jasmine   Not really.

Abeni   Seriously? People never ask you what 'on fleek' means or if you can twerk? Like, dude – I'm from Manchester, not the Bronx.

Jasmine   I dunno. I'd never really thought about it. Anyway, you can twerk. I saw you do it in Love Shack.

Abeni   So? I thought it was funny, so I learned. Anyone can.

Jasmine   I can't. I just kind of squat and twitch. Like . . . (*She demonstrates.*)

Abeni   Wait wait wait, let me open my camera/

Jasmine   No! That secret dies with me.

Abeni   Come on, Jaz! You've got something special. Show the world your sexy twitch.

Abeni *mimics* **Jasmine***'s twerking and both girls get the giggles. An indistinct voice from offstage makes them stop abruptly.*

Abeni   Oh – sorry – we're just looking. Thanks.

Jasmine   We're gonna get kicked out of the hair shop.

Abeni   It's fine, chill.

Jasmine   I came in here once before, ages ago. Got the train in especially and left totally bewildered. I don't even know what half these products are.

Abeni   You can just ask.

Jasmine   I know, I'm just funny about asking for help. I feel like I should know. Did two laps of the shop and bolted out the door, totally confused. And then . . .

Abeni   And then what?

Jasmine   Nothing.

Abeni   So . . . obviously something.

Jasmine   And then as I was walking down to the station, this man walked past me and . . . It was really weird.

Abeni   What? Ew, did he flash you?

Jasmine   No! He said 'nig nog'.

Abeni   *Excuse me?*

Jasmine   Yeah. But quiet, like he was just letting me know.

Abeni   Wow. I'm so sorry.

Jasmine   Thanks. It's OK.

Abeni   That is just . . .

Jasmine   Really old school.

Abeni   Vintage racism.

Jasmine   Sounds like a biscuit.

Abeni (*laughing*)   Cup of tea and a nig nog, Jasmine?

Jasmine   Don't mind if I do, Abeni.

Abeni   I'm so sorry, babe. So what happened? No one said anything?

Jasmine   No one else heard.

Abeni   Wow. Welcome to the North East.

Jasmine   Whey no, it's not like that.

Abeni   If it happened, it's like that.

Jasmine   No, it's not – People are nice up here. It's friendly.

Abeni   Oh yeah, just your friendly neighbourhood racist.

Jasmine   You get them everywhere.

Abeni   Yeah, but they don't usually get to walk away without *at least* getting an earful. Zero tolerance, Jaz. No one gets to do that to you.

Jasmine   I did tell him to go fuck himself. People stared.

Abeni   Yes, OK! Don't mess with Jasmine.

Jasmine   I'm not normally like that.

Abeni   Yeah, maybe not. You couldn't even watch that boxing match.

Jasmine   They were hitting each other on purpose!

Abeni   They're big lads, Jaz. They can handle it. Plus – Anthony Joshua.

Jasmine   Oh my god, yes! He is *lush*. So tall and just all . . . (*Tries to mime the shape of a muscly man.*)

Abeni   I don't need convincing, I'm in. He's a snack.

Jasmine   A whole entire meal. (*Pause.*) It just made me really angry. I just kept thinking – that is so unfair. I'm nice to everyone. I'm the most inoffensive person ever.

Abeni   That's never going to be good enough for some people.

Jasmine   I know. So why do I care?

Abeni   Because you're normal? Everyone cares about that stuff. But remember – you're better than him.

Jasmine   Yeah. Thanks, Abi.

Abeni   Come on, focus up. Hair. Purple hair for purple braids . . . Sexy purple braids for the fierce new Jasmine, twitching and twerking in Love Shack . . .?

Jasmine   No.

Abeni   Alright. That is one thing about living up here – the nightlife is pretty good. And cheap. I kind of get why Mum is so nostalgic about going to uni here. My grandparents are pretty conservative, super protective. She basically went from modest clothes and Bible study to hotpants and tequila slammers up North Road.

Jasmine   I can't imagine your mam being wild. She's so proper.

Abeni   Well yeah, she's all grown up now. Thank god.

Jasmine   So why'd she want to move back?

Abeni   For the good job. For a change of scene. After Dad.

Jasmine   Oh. Yeah. Sorry.

Pause.

Abeni   No, it's fine. (*Consciously changing the subject.*) So what look were you going for?

Jasmine   Honestly, I'm not going for anything. I just started looking at pictures of afro hairstyles online and found all these *amazing* pics of Black girls with purple braids, and I just . . . I really, really wanted those braids.

Abeni   So why the hesitation now?

Jasmine   It just feels a bit fake. Like I'm dressing up as someone else.

Abeni   So? That's all most people are doing.

Jasmine   I know. You're right.

Abeni   You don't need permission to look cool or whatever.

Jasmine   No, I know. It's not that.

Abeni   Oh my god, am I giving you the Mum Lectures?

Jasmine   I mean . . .

Abeni   I am. I'm giving you the Lectures.

Jasmine   I kind of envy you with your mam.

Abeni   Really? But your mum seems lovely. She's all, 'call me Louise', and giving me lifts and advice about college. Always feeding me.

Jasmine   You like anyone who gives you food. You're like a dog.

Abeni   Oi! Cheeky bish.

Jasmine   It's a compliment! Dogs are awesome.

Abeni   Still. Put some respeck on my name, yeah?

Jasmine   I just mean, Mam always struggled with my hair. I remember having to sit while she *dragged* a brush through it, and I was crying, and she was crying . . . She wouldn't let us wear it, like, *out* in case it got tangled. It was always in plaits. I once had a *massive* row with her cos I undid my plaits at a sleepover and came home looking like Diana Ross.

Abeni   Is that a bad thing . . .?

Jasmine   I didn't think so, but she was not best suited. We had words. It just seemed really unfair. All the other girls had their hair out.

Abeni   Is your hair really kinky then? I just assumed you'd have, like, looser curls.

Jasmine   I don't know, to be honest. I've had it relaxed since . . . well, forever.

Abeni   So what about your dad?

Jasmine   Wasn't around. I was dead little when he left. I don't really remember him.

Abeni   Are you still in touch with his family?

Jasmine   Never was. I don't think Mam got along with them, to be honest.

Abeni   You're literally the only Black person in your family?

Jasmine   Yeah.

Abeni   Wow. So do you talk to your Mum about, like, Black people stuff?

Jasmine   Like what?

Abeni   I don't know. Racism at school, or where you're from-from or whatever.

Jasmine   I'm from Durham.

Abeni   Yeah, course, but . . . What about when some weirdo gives you abuse in the street?

Jasmine   To be honest . . . I don't tell her that stuff.

Abeni   She's your mum, you should tell her.

Jasmine   No, I know. I used to ask questions sometimes, but it was always a bit awkward so I stopped. 'You're not Black, you're not White, you're just Jasmine.' She said that a lot.

Abeni   Well that sucks.

Jasmine   Does it? Maybe I like being an ethnicity of one.

Pause.

Abeni   Jaz, do you really think you're not Black?

Jasmine   No, I know I am. Kind of. Just not *black* Black.

Abeni   What's *black* Black?

Jasmine   Like, fully, properly Black. I don't know! It's just something people say, isn't it?

Abeni   Not to me. Anyway, who's saying that?

Jasmine Just . . . people.

Abeni That's messed up. What's wrong with being Black?

Jasmine I don't think that's what they mean. It's more like, they see me as being like them. Like they can identify, or something.

Abeni They can't do that without pretending you're white?

Jasmine I don't think it's supposed to be an insult.

Abeni Maybe, but I'm insulted, and *you* should be. They're basically saying it's better not to be what you are.

Jasmine What am I, though? I don't feel Black. I think about all the other Black people out there and they all seem so . . .

Pause.

Abeni What?

Jasmine Connected. A part of something. A part of their heritage, a part of a community. I don't know any other Black people apart from you, and I only met you a couple of months ago. I'm not connected.

Abeni No, but . . . You've met me now. That's a start.

Jasmine I know. But still . . . we're different.

Abeni And so is every other Black person out there. Different in millions of ways. You don't have to fit some stereotype. Just be you, in brown skin. That's enough.

Jasmine Yeah.

Abeni That old man knew you were Black. He saw you. And that's fine, because I see you, too. You're gorgeous and sweet and a bit weird and you're Black. (*Pause*) I think purple braids could say that.

Jasmine Yeah?

Abeni Yeah. So are we doing this?

Jasmine (*firm*)   Yes.

Abeni   Are you sure? Because I'm going to call the lady back over here and she is going to sell you at least six bags of purple hair.

Jasmine   Yes. We're doing it.

Abeni   Yes! I swear to god, you are going to look *so peng*. Let's buy some hair. 'Scuse me . . .

Scene Two

December 2017. The following Monday. A quiet corner of the college campus. **Jasmine** *sits on the kerb or ground, huddled up hugging her knees. She's wearing a hat pulled as far over her head as she can, her braids tucked into her coat. Enter* **Abeni**.

Abeni   There you are. I thought we was getting lunch?

Jasmine   Yeah. I'm not that hungry.

Abeni   Well I am. Come on, I'll get you a coffee.

Jasmine   Nah. I'm just gonna chill here for a bit.

Abeni   What? (*Pause.*) What's going on?

Jasmine   What? Nothing. I'm just, you know . . .

Abeni   No, I don't know. What's with the hat? It's not that cold.

Jasmine   It is a bit.

Pause.

Abeni   You hate the braids.

Jasmine (*standing*)   No! No, I love them. I do.

Abeni   You're embarrassed about them. Listen, we can take them down –

Jasmine   No! I just . . . I'm having an adjustment period.

Abeni (*dubious*)   Right.

Jasmine   I'm just really aware of them. On my head.

Abeni   Yeah. That is where they are.

Jasmine   Like a big flashing sign saying '*look at me*'.

Abeni   OK? But you knew people would see them at some point.

Jasmine   I was trying not to think about that part.

Abeni   Good. Don't think about it, just get on with it. Come on.

She snatches **Jasmine**'s *hat and goes to walk off.* **Jasmine** *tries to grab it back.*

Jasmine   Hey!

Abeni   Oh, come on, Jaz! Look, we can take them out tonight if you want but for today, you're just going to have to deal with it.

Jasmine   No, that's worse. Purple braids one day, wussing out the next. Anyway, I don't want to take them out. I'm just, you know.

Abeni (*impatient*)   What?

Jasmine   I don't know, I'm nervous. I'm not like you.

Abeni   Not like me how?

Jasmine   Not all confident and outgoing. You don't care what anyone thinks. You're all cool.

Abeni (*scornful*)   Cool. Of course I care.

Jasmine   You do not!

Abeni   *Of course I care.* I just try not to let it stop me. But yeah, I care.

Jasmine   You do a really good job of hiding it.

Abeni   Fake it till you feel it. Look, I do know what you mean. I still feel like I stand out here.

Jasmine   Yeah, but in a good way. People love your whole . . . thing. Your unique style.

Abeni   Not unique. I'm totally normal.

Jasmine   But you're different round here. Good different, not weird different.

Abeni   I don't even know what that means.

Jasmine   You're cool.

Abeni *groans, exasperated.*

Abeni   Let's do a role play. What do you think people are going to say about the braids?

Jasmine   You're joking.

Abeni   I'm not. Let's think up some comebacks. What's a comment you're expecting?

Jasmine   Well, Mam said they were a bit unprofessional.

Abeni   Unprofessional? What, are you an accountant now?

Jasmine   No, but I'm looking for a weekend job, and she just thought/

Abeni   Greggs aren't gonna care, Jaz. I promise.

Jasmine   Yeah, I think she just doesn't want to admit she hates them.

Abeni   That's parents init. She'll get used to it. Anyway, no one at college is gonna be like, 'Oh Jasmine, those braids are so unprofessional'. So come on. What kind of things are you expecting?

Jasmine   I don't know, do I? I never know until they say it and then my mind goes blank and I'm just stood there like *duh*.

Abeni   You talk like this happens all the time.

Jasmine   It does. Or it did, for a while. You know – you wear the wrong thing to a disco, or your mam gets you some shit knock-off trainers, and that's all you hear about for ages after.

Abeni   Seriously? Is fashion a big deal in Durham?

Jasmine (*laughing*)   Shut up, you know what I mean. And especially hair . . . I never got hair right. (*Pause*) Once, me mam tried straightening my hair at home and I think she left it on too long cos loads of it broke off and it was just really dry and frizzy and these two lads started calling us 'pubes'.

Abeni *clamps a hand over her mouth, tries not to laugh.*

Jasmine   Yeah. That was fun. First week of secondary school.

Abeni (*still laughing a bit*)   Babes. That sucks. But that was secondary school. That's done. You're in college now, new crowd. No one remembers that shit.

Jasmine   Some people might. But it's more like . . . I just don't want the attention.

Abeni   Jaz, this is totally different. You look awesome. Seriously. You look *lush*, as people say up here.

Jasmine   Well. Thanks.

Abeni   Just stick with me and if anyone gives you shit, I'll rip them a new one.

Jasmine   Yeah?

Abeni   Yeah.

Jasmine   Thanks. I can't believe you're friends with me.

Abeni   Why?

Jasmine   Cos. (*Mocking.*) You're cool.

Abeni   There's that word again.

Jasmine   You are though! Why don't you like it?

Abeni   It's just, I'm not. I'm normal. I'm OK with just being normal. And I don't even think it is the cool thing, it's more like – Are you an amazing singer? Are you dead sporty? Do you love spicy food? Do you speak African? How many times have you seen *Black Panther?* Who's your favourite in it? You're so *urban,* you're so *sassy,* you're so *cool.*

Jasmine   OK . . .

Abeni   Sometimes I think, I should dress different, blend in a bit, but what's the point? I'll still stick out like a sore thumb. Besides, I won't even be here in a few months.

Jasmine   Why?

Abeni   Cos. I'll finish the year, get my A-levels, move on. Probably go back home, get a job down there.

Jasmine   Course. Yeah.

Abeni   And none of this will matter. And you'll move on too, off to uni. You probably won't even see most of these people again, unless you want to. So why worry what they think?

Jasmine   I don't know. Habit, I 'spose. (*Pause.*) Do you really think you'll move back to Manchester after college?

Abeni   I mean, probably. Won't be anything keeping me here.

Jasmine   What about your mam?

Abeni   She'll be fine. She *is* fine. She's already settled in, with church and everything. We don't see that much of each other anyway. And she'd want me to be happy, so . . . (*Shrugs.*)

Jasmine   Are you on your own loads then?

Abeni   Quite a bit, I 'spose. I don't mind.

Jasmine   You can always come over to mine. I'm hardly ever doing anything.

Abeni   Thanks. But it's fine, honestly. I like my own company.

Jasmine   Are you . . . are you not close to your mam?

Abeni   We're close. We just like different things.

Jasmine (*hesitant, worried she's crossing a line*)   Were . . . Were you close to your dad?

Pause.

Abeni   Yeah. Yeah, I was.

Jasmine   So are you . . .? I just mean, how . . . Sorry.

Abeni   Nah, it's fine. I miss him. We both do. Mum . . . everyone grieves in their own way, I suppose. She's got church. She cleans a lot, and cries when she thinks I won't notice. Sometimes she cleans and cries at the same time. Multitasking.

Jasmine   What about you? I'm sorry I know / we don't . . .

Abeni   Nah, it's fine. Honestly. I can talk about it, there's just not much to say.

Pause. **Jasmine** *ever-so-casually reaches for the hat* **Abeni** *is still holding.* **Abeni** *whisks it away.*

Abeni   No you don't. Come on, we're doing this.

Jasmine   'We.' *I'm* doing it. You're fine.

Abeni   *You're* fine. You're making a big deal of it. No one's gonna call you pubes now, are they?

Jasmine   I should never have told you that. (*Deep breath.*) Come on, then. I could fancy some chips.

Abeni   Yes! Chips and curry sauce.

Jasmine   And cheese.

Abeni   Ew! Curry sauce and cheese? You pervert.

Jasmine   You should try it. It's *lush*.

They both start to walk away.

Abeni   I'm not sure I wanna be seen with someone eating that.

Jasmine   Come on, Abi. Who cares what people think, right?

They walk away.

Scene Three

January 2018. Just after Christmas. Durham Cathedral – a college visit. A tour has just concluded. **Jasmine** *is taking pictures with her phone.* **Abeni** *wanders nearby, hugging herself for warmth.*

Abeni   What are you even taking pictures of?

Jasmine   Just . . . whatever. Pillars and carvings and stuff.

Abeni   Are we gonna need that?

Jasmine   No idea.

Abeni *shuffles, trying to warm up.*

Abeni   Can we go and sit in the café?

Jasmine   You really not interested at all?

Abeni   I'm just freezing. How is it this cold? We're indoors.

Jasmine   It's a big space. (*Looking up.*) Imagine designing this. Imagine sitting down and making a load of plans and working out how you're gonna put a roof on this *massive* cathedral, the whole time knowing you'll be dead before it's even finished.

Abeni   Well, yeah. Life expectancy was, like, thirty. So you could just do some nice, solid foundations, get them sorted while you're alive, and then go full on, balls to the wall with everything else. Just be like, *yeah, throw in a belltower. Let's have a million windows and a MASSIVE vaulted ceiling.* Cos you'd be dead before they got that high anyway.

Jasmine *looks at her.*

Abeni   I've been before. With Mum. Loves a big ol' church, Mum does.

Jasmine   Oh yeah. Mams love a church.

Abeni   Right? And she loves old buildings, so I've been here twice now. Which is how I know that this is the nave and that's the choir, and out there is the cloisters and past *that* is the café where we're gonna get a cup of tea and warm up.

Jasmine   Still. Why'd you come twice?

Abeni   I dunno, Mum wanted to. And if I don't tag along on her little day trips, half the time I don't even see her.

Jasmine   That's a bit . . .

Abeni (*a little challenging*)   What?

Jasmine (*cautious*)   Sad?

Abeni   Yeah, it is. We're just . . . Christmas was not fun. I really wish we'd gone back home but Mum wanted to stay here, and I didn't want to leave her on her own, but then . . . It was just bleak.

Jasmine   Was that your first Christmas without your dad?

Abeni   Second. But we were at Aunty Pat's last year, there was loads of us. Big family thing. This year it was just me and Mum staring at each other across the table with nothing to say to each other.

Jasmine   I'm so sorry. I wish you'd said, you could've joined forces with us. It was just me and Mam as well, but that's normal. We watched a lot of rom-coms.

Abeni   That sounds like a different kind of bleak, to be honest.

Jasmine   Don't know what you're missing. (*Looking up and around.*) I love this cathedral. Makes us feel . . . like . . . proud, or something. Like, that's mine. I've got a share in that.

Abeni   Sure.

Jasmine   You think I'm daft.

Abeni   Nah, nah. I get it. But, you know . . . I'm not from Durham, am I? It's just another big old church to me. It's a good one, don't get me wrong. And that there, that's a nice window. But once you've seen it two or three times . . . (*Shrugs.*)

Jasmine   Alright, I can see I'm not about to get you all fired up about the cathedral today.

Abeni   Shit.

She dodges back to hide from someone, pulling **Jasmine** *with her.*

Jasmine   What?

Abeni   Shush!

Jasmine   Why? Who are we hiding from?

Abeni   That girl. What's her name?! Blonde, big earrings.

Jasmine (*dismayed*)   Oh. Katie Bell.

Abeni   Yeah-yeah, her.

Jasmine   What's she done?

They both poke their heads out, then quickly pull back again.

Abeni   She cornered me this morning when we were waiting for the bus.

Jasmine   What for?

Abeni   She heard I did these init. (*Lifting some of* **Jasmine**'s *braids.*) Now she wants some and all.

Jasmine   But you don't want to do them.

Abeni   Nah. And I told her that, but she's not taking no for an answer. If she hassles me again she's gonna get banged out.

Jasmine   Can't you give her a reason?

Abeni   I mean . . . it takes ages. Time and effort. But mainly I just . . . I don't want her to have them.

Jasmine   No.

Abeni   It's stupid. It's not like box braids are something sacred or whatever.

Jasmine   No. No, of course not. Not really. But . . .

They look at each other, grimacing and cringing a little.

Abeni   It does feel a bit wrong.

Jasmine   A bit . . . inappropriate? And kind of . . . unfair?

Abeni   Yeah! Like – can we not just have this one thing? Just for us?

Jasmine   Just let us have this.

Abeni   Just this one thing. Can't say that, though.

Jasmine   Oh, no.

Abeni   So she's getting a flat *no*.

Jasmine   OK, but . . . try not to rile her up.

Pause. **Abeni** *looks at* **Jasmine** *thoughtfully.*

Abeni   Why?

Jasmine   It's just, she's a bit, you know . . . She might overreact. And it could come back on you.

Abeni   That's all?

Jasmine   Yeah.

Abeni   She talks to you sometimes at college.

Jasmine   So? We're in the same class.

Abeni   Didn't she go to your secondary school?

Jasmine   Yeah.

Abeni   But you're not friends.

Jasmine   No. We hung out in different crowds.

Abeni   And that's it?

Jasmine   That's it.

Abeni   OK. (*Pause.*) Well, fuck her. And fuck this cold. How is the climate *so* different up here? It's like being in another country.

Jasmine   Howay, you soft southerner. It's not that cold.

Abeni (*groans*)   Are we gonna have time for the café? When's the bus leaving?

Jasmine   We've got twenty minutes. Katie's still there, though.

Abeni   Yeah. You know what, I'm just gonna tell her.

Jasmine   No! No, don't.

Abeni   Why? (*Pause.*) Come on, Jaz. You don't like her, do you?

Jasmine (*reluctantly*)   No.

Abeni   How come?

Jasmine   We didn't get along at school, that's all.

Abeni   She was a bully.

Jasmine   Kind of. She never beat us up or anything. It was just this one thing.

Abeni   One bad thing.

Jasmine   It was ages ago. Year eight. It was about me dad.

Abeni   Was your dad around then?

Jasmine   No. That was kind of the point. She started a rumour about him. That Mam left him cos he had ebola. So it was all, *stay away from Jasmine, she's got ebola.*

Abeni   *Excuse me?*

Jasmine   I know. It was so stupid, it didn't even make any sense. No one believed it, not really.

Abeni   Well, yeah. It's obvious bullshit.

Jasmine   Oh yeah. But loads of people acted like it was a real thing. So it didn't matter that it was bullshit. They still treated us like I was, like I was . . .

Abeni   Babes.

Jasmine   Yeah. And I kind of – I kind of think it was her dad who actually started it. She said it was him what told her, so he probably told a shitty joke at home and then she comes into school and . . .

Abeni   Jaz. That sucks.

Jasmine   Yeah. It didn't actually go on for that long, but it kind of set the tone, you know? I was a target for everything after that. And that was it for secondary school.

Abeni   I had no idea.

Jasmine   I never tell anyone. And I'm always weirded out when she tries to talk to us at college. It's like she doesn't even remember.

Abeni   She probably doesn't. Nothing to her, is it?

Jasmine   Yeah.

Abeni   There's no way I'm doing her hair now. Not after she messed with my girl.

Jasmine   Thanks, Abz.

Abeni   No problem, babes. You know, I can do you one better. I'm gonna tell Katie Bell to go fuck herself.

Jasmine   No, don't!

Abeni   Look, she's still there. (*Moving away.*) Katie!

Jasmine   *Abi!*

Abeni   Can I have a word?

Jasmine   NO!

Abeni *goes after* **Katie Bell** *and* **Jasmine** *follows*.

Scene Four

March 2018. Just before Easter. **Jasmine** *and* **Abeni** *sit in a pub garden in a Durham pit village.*

Abeni   This is perfect.

Jasmine   I didn't even know this pub was here.

Abeni   Yeah, Mum brought me here for lunch last week. I thought it was nice, a bit more chill than town.

Jasmine   It is. It's very out of the way. I thought you hated being out in the country? You're always complaining about how quiet it is at home.

Abeni   That's different though! It's weird! I get the creeps. Like, sometimes there's literally no one else on the street. And then when you do see someone, they say *hello* and start chatting, like they know you! It's so weird.

Jasmine   You just need to get used to it.

Abeni   Bruv. It's been months. It's not happening. Night-time's the weirdest. When it's dark that field at the back of the house is like, *really dark*. Pitch black. Like, anything could be hiding out there. Anything.

Jasmine   Not anything. Not like we've got bears or wolves or anything.

Abeni   You've never seen *Jeepers Creepers*, have you?

Jasmine *is laughing at her.*

Abeni   I'm serious! Nothing good ever came crawling out of a field.

Jasmine   There's loads of people would love to live out here. I'd love to live out here.

Abeni   You would not.

Jasmine   I would! (*Pause.*) Well, one day, I would.

Abeni   Yeah, but not right now when you've got a life.

Jasmine*'s phone beeps.*

Jasmine   Not much of a life. Going to college, going to work, hanging out with you. And in a couple of months there'll be no college, and you keep threatening to leave . . .

Jasmine*'s phone beeps.*

Abeni   You're popular. What am I missing?

Jasmine   It's just this girl from work. She's out in town, she's hassling me to come along. I've told her I'm not up for it.

Abeni   Oh. Right.

Jasmine   I don't feel like a big night.

Abeni   Don't let me stop you.

Jasmine   No, no, it's fine. This is nice.

Abeni   How is the job?

Jasmine   It's alright, yeah. The people are canny. I miss my weekends, though.

Abeni   Yeah, but at least you're not skint all the time. (*Pause.*) So this girl that's out in town –

Jasmine   Paris.

Abeni   Paris? So is she one of the *canny* ones?

Jasmine   Oh yeah. She's awesome. Really fun.

Abeni   Yeah? Cool.

Jasmine   Not as much fun as you.

Abeni (*laughing*)   It's fine, you're allowed to have more than one friend.

Jasmine   Course. She is lovely. You should meet her.

Abeni (*lying, overcompensating*)   Yeah, I'd love that.

Jasmine   Yeah. Cool. (*Pause.*) We should do more of this over the summer. Go out to the coast or something.

Abeni   Coast sounds good. We'll have to do it before my trip home. We need to redo your braids as well. You're getting scruffy again.

Jasmine   Actually, I'm thinking about going natural.

Abeni   Why? Your mum been on at you about them?

Jasmine   No, I just want to try it. And my roots have already grown in quite a bit.

Abeni   Oh, OK. I can help you take them down then.

Jasmine   We could both do it! Go natural for the summer.

Abeni   I am natural. What do you think is growing out of my head?

Jasmine   You know what I mean. You'd look so cool with a massive afro.

Abeni   All the time? Nah. Too much work.

Jasmine   Is it? Washing it would be easier than washing around braids.

Abeni   For you, maybe.

Jasmine   Why for me?

Abeni   Cos. You've got loose curls. Mine's tighter, detangling is a proper ball-ache. Hours, sometimes. Don't need more of that in my life.

Jasmine   Yeah. I just thought it might look good.

Abeni   It would look amazing. It's just not for me.

Jasmine   Fair enough. Paris is really into it, she's given me a few tips already.

Abeni   Ah, got it. She's a militant naturalista. All Malcolm X and coconut oil. (*Malcolm X voice.*) 'Who taught you to hate the texture of your hair?'

Jasmine (*laughing*)   She's actually got that quote on her Instagram. But she's not militant, she's just . . . passionate. You should see her Instagram, she does all sorts with it. Here.

Abeni   Oh yeah. Is she . . . is she mixed?

Jasmine   Yeah. Her mam's from Ethiopia. She was telling us about the history of hair in Ethiopia, how dreadlocks started there as an act of resistance. She's really into it.

Abeni   Yeah, see, her hair's not that curly. Yours is definitely tighter than that.

Jasmine   Still. I think it'll be fine.

Abeni   You'll find out when you do the chop. As long as you're doing it for you.

Jasmine (*a bit miffed*)   Of course. I'm not just copying the cool girl.

Abeni   I didn't say that. I'm just saying, it's not one size fits all. You should totally change things up if you want to.

Jasmine   I feel like I've given the wrong impression of her.

Abeni   No, don't worry. If you say she's nice, I believe you.

Pause.

Jasmine   You could come into town and meet her.

Abeni   You're going then.

Jasmine   No, I just mean, if you wanted to meet her, we could go into town.

Abeni   I'm not really up for a big night.

Jasmine   It doesn't have to be. I think it'll be fun. And it wouldn't hurt you to meet more people.

Abeni   Um, OK. I'm fine, really. But you should go if you want to.

Jasmine   No, I'd rather hang out with you. It was just a suggestion.

Pause.

Abeni   I could come for a couple. Just say hi.

Jasmine   Yeah? I'm not up for a big night either. We can just swing by, have a couple, get a pizza and head home.

Abeni (*still unsure*)   Yeah. Sounds good.

Jasmine   You sure?

Abeni   Yeah. Why not.

Jasmine   OK then. I'll check buses. Eee we're gannen oot!

Scene Five

March 2018. The morning after. **Jasmine** *and* **Abeni** *are asleep top-to-toe in* **Jasmine**'s *bed.*

Jasmine *wakes up with a gasp.*

Jasmine   OH MY GOD.

Abeni (*from under the covers*)   I KNOW!

Jasmine (*groaning*)   Oh. My. God.

Abeni (*slowly sitting up*)   I know.

Jasmine   My mouth tastes like, like . . .

Abeni   Like arse.

Jasmine   Yeah.

Abeni (*pulling a pizza box from under the covers*)   Want some pizza? Cleanse your palate.

Jasmine (*gagging*)   No.

Abeni   What time did we get in?

Jasmine   There's a text message for a taxi – 4 am.

Abeni   And I think we were up for a bit after we got back here. Oh god, your Mum was up.

Jasmine   Oh yeah, she was! She was not happy. There's a picture of us outside the Fighting Cocks – did we go in the Fighting Cocks?

Abeni   No, you just thought the name was hilarious. Where's my phone?

Jasmine (*sniggering to herself*)   Oh yeah.

Abeni   Found it.

Jasmine   Pizza shop . . . Shots . . . Wetherspoons . . .

Abeni   Can't believe I let you drag me into a 'Spoons. And it was *extra sticky* last night. And there was that girl fight in there!

Jasmine   Oh my god, that's right! And the bouncers were just stood there watching.

Abeni   Then they were in the pizza shop an hour later sharing a meat feast.

Jasmine   All mates again! Like it never happened!

Abeni   I know! Mad.

Jasmine (*disgusted*)   I've got a picture of a pint glass full of puke.

She tries to show it to **Abeni**, *who gags and pushes the phone away.*

Abeni   I've got a picture of a dick.

She shows the picture to **Jasmine**.

Jasmine   Why's it so angry?

Abeni   No idea. (*Beat.*) What happened with that ginger dude? You disappeared with him for ages.

Jasmine   Oh! *That* guy! (*Amused.*) We did have a bit of a snog on, but then he wanted us to go home with him and he kept saying, 'I've never been with a coloured lass' and I was like, you know what, I'm gonna let it slide because he was a good kisser and I did fancy him, but he said it again, so I was like, well that's OK because I've never been with a ginger and he got *so annoyed*.

Abeni   Why?

Jasmine   Oh, he's so sick of ginger jokes, especially since he's not even really ginger, he's more strawberry blonde –

Abeni   He was ginger!

Jasmine   Mate! His arm hair was orange. But he's *so sick* of that being the one thing people comment on –

Abeni   Mate.

Jasmine   And I was like – yeah. Dude. Listen to yourself. I couldn't stop laughing, I think that pissed him off more than anything.

Abeni   So he still hasn't been with a 'coloured lass'.

Jasmine   Nope. Who knows what he was expecting.

Abeni   Acrobatics and a fireworks display.

Jasmine   Thought I was gonna backflip right onto his dick. It hurts to laugh. I need tablets.

Abeni   Jaz?

Jasmine   What?

Abeni   I feel like your mum was giving me evils last night.

Jasmine   She was giving us both evils. We're not . . . things are bit off at the minute.

Abeni   How come?

Jasmine   Do you remember the first time you came over and braided me hair? And I told you about that man outside the hair shop?

Abeni   That gave you abuse? Yeah.

Jasmine   And you were the first person I'd told. I never even told Mam.

Abeni   Yeah.

Jasmine   Well, a couple of weeks ago, I thought – I'm gonna tell her. I should tell her.

Abeni   And?

Jasmine   It was a nightmare. She asked loads of questions, wanted to really get to the bottom of what was wrong with this man. Was he old, senile? Was he drunk? Was he acting strange? Had I said something to him? And I was like – *no*. There was nothing wrong with him. He was just racist. She did not want to accept it and I got annoyed, told her she was calling us a liar, she got all up a height . . . I just wanted her to say 'I'm sorry that happened to you'.

Abeni   Babes. That's rough. But don't stop telling her that stuff.

Jasmine   Yeah. It just feels like she doesn't want to talk about. She thinks I've changed since you and me started hanging out. Like you're getting us all worked up about stuff.

Abeni   *What?* How is it my fault? Coz I said you should tell her?

Jasmine   I 'spose. She thinks I'm just doing whatever you tell me. So. That's why things are all awkward.

Abeni   You'll get past it.

Jasmine   I hope so. At least the braids won't be in much longer. One less thing to argue about.

Abeni   You *are* changing your hair to keep your mum happy.

Jasmine   I'm not! That's just an added bonus.

Abeni   Fair enough. Maybe I'll change it up myself. Get locs or twists or shave it all off.

Jasmine   I don't think I could pull off bald.

Abeni   Don't tell your mate Paris. She'll have a whole speech about how liberating it is and everyone should try it once.

Jasmine   You really can't stand her.

Abeni   It's not like that. She's just not my kind of people.

Jasmine   Who is? You only hang out with me.

Abeni   What are you saying?

Jasmine   I don't know. You could be a bit more open.

Abeni   What for? I just want to finish college and go home. Promise I'll miss you though.

Jasmine   Thanks, pet. You never know, you might move back down south and suddenly find you miss Durham.

Abeni   I mean, anything is possible. I know I won't miss being *the* Black girl.

Jasmine   Yeah, me neither.

Abeni (*amused*)   Yeah, not quite the same thing.

Jasmine   Cos I'm local.

Abeni (*grudgingly*)   Yeah . . . It's just generally . . . different.

Jasmine (*irritated*)   What are you on about?

Abeni   Nah, it's just . . . People don't look at us the same way, do they?

Jasmine   Do they not?

Abeni   You know they don't. You said yourself, people don't see you as *black* Black.

Jasmine   And you said that was bullshit.

Abeni   It's a bullshit thing for people to think and say, but they still act on it and that's reality. Trust me, they look at me and they see *black* Black.

Jasmine   OK, but it's not like they're looking at me and saying, *oh look, there goes another white person*. It doesn't stop us getting the shit stuff. Random abuse in the street.

Abeni   Yeah, but . . .

Jasmine   What?

Abeni (*frustrated*)   It's not the same, Jaz.

Jasmine   OK, like what?

Abeni   Like at college. Miss Gardiner.

Jasmine   She's strict with everyone.

Abeni   Yeah, but she's not telling everyone their earrings are *ghetto fabulous*.

Jasmine   Well, yeah. That was a bit ignorant / but –

Abeni   Right when I started at college, I got a C on an assignment and she congratulated me on catching up. And when told her I was getting As and Bs before, she laughed at me. She thinks I'm stupid.

Jasmine   I don't / think she –

Abeni   If I put my hand up, she just ignores me. I haven't answered a single question in her class. She basically gives me no feedback on my work, but she's always got comments about what I'm wearing. The way I talk. (*Pause.*) You *know* she's weird with me. All the time. But she's fine with you. See? Different.

Jasmine   Fine. It's different.

Abeni   Don't be touchy about it. I'm just sayin' –

Jasmine   No, it's fine. Sorry I don't get as much shit as you, I suppose.

Abeni   Oh, don't do that. I'm just saying what's on my mind.

Jasmine   Right. Cos it kind of feels like you're having a go at us.

Abeni   I am not having a go at you. Pointing out that our skin tones are different, and that therefore things in general are different for us, is not *having a go*.

Jasmine   I just don't see why it matters if our experiences aren't *exactly* the same.

Abeni   Because! It's not just different flavours of the same thing, it's a whole other level of bullshit. Nobody's saying light-skinned girls are loud. Angry. Aggressive. Unfeminine. You're the acceptable version of blackness.

Jasmine   That is –! *I* don't think that!

Abeni   *I know.* You asked how it's different. That's how.

Jasmine   OK, but I don't get how it's my fault.

Abeni   (*exasperated*)   God, Jaz! It's not your fault. I'm not asking you to fix it.

Jasmine Then why are you so riled up?

Abeni *Because!* This – you – doing this.

Jasmine Doing what?

Abeni Oh, for fuck's sake. Forget I said anything.

Jasmine No, come on. Get it off your chest.

Abeni It's not like that, Jaz. I'm trying to tell you something, something about me, about *being me*, and you're making it about you. Can you just listen?

Long pause.

Jasmine Yeah.

Abeni I'm not saying it to make you feel less . . . whatever.

Jasmine No.

Abeni I want to be able to talk to you about that stuff.

Jasmine Yeah. OK.

Abeni Really?

Jasmine Yeah. It's fine. (*It's not fine.*)

Pause.

Abeni Maybe I should go home.

Jasmine Yeah. Maybe.

Abeni Right. I'll text you.

Jasmine Sure.

Abeni *exits.*

Scene Six

*June 2018, a few weeks after their argument. A clothes shop – a couple of messy racks, clothes on the floor. **Abeni** is tidying up. She's wearing staff ID on a lanyard. She's hunkered down, picking things up off the floor, when **Jasmine** enters and starts going through the* *other rack of clothes.* **Jasmine***'s braids are now silver-grey.* **Abeni** *stands and they both see each other, stop dead.*

Abeni (*surprised*)   Jasmine.

Jasmine (*fake surprised*)   Oh my god, Abi! Do you work here?

Abeni   What? / Yeah –

Jasmine   I was just –

Pause. She grabs a random item of clothing.

. . . browsing. (*Pause.*) You've got a job.

Abeni (*obviously!?*)   Yeah . . .

Jasmine (*nervous laugh*)   Obviously.

Quite long, awkward pause. **Abeni** *turns back to her work.*

Jasmine (*a bit too loud*)   How's your mam?

Beat.

Abeni   Fine.

Jasmine   Good. I'm glad. (*Pause.*) I'm doing alright.

Abeni   OK. Look, I'm working/

Jasmine   Yeah! Yeah, of course.

Jasmine *doesn't leave.* **Abeni** *continues her task.*

Jasmine   This seems like a decent place to work. You get a discount?

Silence.

You'd need it. Look at these prices.

Silence. **Jasmine** *looks even more unsure of herself.*

Nice clothes, though.

Silence.

Manager (*indistinct, from off*)   Abeni! Can you come to the counter, please?

Abeni *sighs heavily and exits.*

Jasmine *stands, unsure whether to leave, then continues* **Abeni**'s *tidying. Spends a minute or so tidying the racks while she waits.* **Abeni** *reenters, watches* **Jasmine** *for a moment. Shakes her head.*

Abeni   You don't need to do that.

Jasmine   Right.

Abeni *continues tidying.*

Abeni (*snaps*)   What are you doing here?

Jasmine   I'm just/

Abeni   Don't say shopping, you're not shopping. What are you doing here?

Jasmine   I'm . . . I was . . . I walked past a couple of days ago and saw you in the window. Straddling a mannequin.

She mimes it, trying to make a joke. **Abeni** *doesn't respond.* **Jasmine** *gives up.*

Jasmine   You won't talk to me at college. Don't even say hello. I just thought, if I came here . . .

Abeni   What? You'd have me cornered and I'd be forced to talk to you? Yeah. Well. Looks like it worked. What do you want?

Jasmine   I want . . . I want us to be talking.

Abeni   About . . .?

Jasmine   About anything. Like before.

Abeni   Before what?

Jasmine   You know. Before . . . when you stayed at mine, and we . . .

Abeni   Had that argument?

Jasmine   Yeah.

Abeni   I wanted to talk. That's why I texted you the next day.

Jasmine (*sheepish*)   Yeah.

Abeni   And the day after.

Jasmine   Yeah.

Abeni   And again after that. No reply. How come? (*Pause.*) You should try being a bit braver, Jaz. You might actually get somewhere.

Jasmine   I thought . . . I was still angry for a bit. I thought you were angry, too.

Abeni   I was. But we still could've talked about it.

Jasmine   I thought we would just keep arguing. And I was scared that if that happened . . .

Pause.

Abeni   What?

Jasmine   That if that happened, you'd ditch us.

Abeni   Ditch you?

Jasmine   Yeah. Like, that would be it.

Abeni   I wouldn't – It's not like – It wasn't *that* bad.

Jasmine   Then why aren't you talking to us?

Abeni   Because! I texted you, like, three or four times and you didn't even bother to reply. I spent the whole Easter holiday stressing over it and then I get back to college and you're trying to act like nothing's happened. (*Pause.*) Pissed me right off.

Jasmine   I didn't really think about it like that. (*Pause.*) Sorry.

Abeni   Yeah. Well. It's done now.

She carries on with her work.

Jasmine (*annoyed*)   It's done? That's it?

Abeni   Yeah.

Jasmine   OK, I messed up/

Abeni   Can you keep your voice down?

Jasmine (*quieter*)   I messed up, but I'm apologising. I want to make it right.

Silence.

Right. Because it's not like you're that bothered anyway, is it?

Abeni   Bothered about what?

Jasmine   About being mates with us. About sorting things out. Cos you're leaving anyway, so why bother.

Abeni   It's not like that/

Jasmine   Cos I was just a stop-gap anyway.

Abeni   That's not true.

Jasmine   Yeah it is. You're always going on about how you can't wait to move back to Manchester.

Abeni   So? That doesn't/

Jasmine   You never would've been mates with us if I'd turned up at your school in Manchester.

Abeni   You don't know that.

Jasmine   I kind of do, though. Are any of your other friends like me?

Abeni   In some ways, yeah.

Jasmine   That's a no.

Abeni   It doesn't matter. You and me did end up friends. Proper friends. (*Pause.*) Pretty much my best friend.

Pause.

Jasmine   Same.

Abeni   Except *you've* got other friends.

Jasmine   I mean, kind of . . . (*Pause. She twigs.*) Is that . . .? Did you think . . . That cos I'd met some people at work . . . It's not like that.

Abeni   I don't know. It just seemed like you and what's-her-face had more in common.

Jasmine   Maybe. In some ways. But I get on better with you.

Abeni *nods, not making eye contact, awkward. Pause.*

Jasmine   Anyway. I'll let you get on. Don't want you to get wrong.

Abeni   Yeah, yeah.

Jasmine   Bye then.

Abeni   Bye.

Jasmine *goes to leave.*

Abeni   Oh my god!

Jasmine (*turning back*)   What?

Abeni   Guess who else works here. An old friend of ours.

Jasmine   Who?

Abeni   Katie Bell.

Jasmine   No!

Abeni   Yep.

Jasmine   Oh god, what's she like?

Abeni   A bitch, obviously. She kept saying how *surprising* it was that they'd taken me on cos I didn't really *fit* their *usual aesthetic*. Then she decided it's cos Black girls are in fashion right now.

Jasmine   Oh, really? What happens when we go out of fashion?

Abeni   Dunno.

Jasmine   But I bet she still wants you to braid her hair.

Abeni   Better. She wanted canerows.

Jasmine   Oh no.

Abeni   Yeah. And I did them.

Jasmine   Oh no. Abi. No.

Abeni   No no no, it's brilliant. She looked *so clapped*. I think they lasted about a week.

Jasmine   Did you get a picture?

Abeni (*taking out her phone*)   Of course.

Jasmine   Oh my god. She looks like she's out on licence. I almost feel sorry for her.

Abeni   She deserved it. (*Pause.*) Look, if you wanted to hang out or whatever . . .

Jasmine   Yeah?

Abeni   Yeah.

Jasmine   Then I will text you. Definitely.

Abeni   Cool. Alright then. Speak soon.

Jasmine   See you.

Jasmine *exits, smiling a little.* **Abeni** *continues tidying.*

Scene Seven

July 2018. Durham town centre. Big Meeting is on – brass bands and crowds carrying banners march through the town. It's sunny, people are drinking. **Abeni** *sits on the grass watching. Enter* **Jasmine**. **Abeni** *stands to greet her.*

Jasmine   Thought I was never gonna find you. It's stowed out.

They hug, a little awkwardly.

Abeni   I know, it's heaving. I spent twenty minutes queuing to use a pub toilet.

Jasmine   At least the sun's out for you.

Abeni   I know! There's gonna be a lot of sunburnt man boobs in Durham at the end of the day.

Jasmine (*laughing*)   Oh god! Just think of all the sad drunk boys at home tonight, rubbing lotion on their nipples.

Abeni   Someone should be handing out factor 50. (*Pause.*) Look at all this.

Jasmine   What? Big Meeting?

Abeni   Yeah. I mean, if I didn't already feel like a foreigner here, this . . .

Jasmine   Oh, come on. It's brass bands. There's nothing exotic about a brass band.

Abeni   But it's the banners, and the marching, and . . . just . . . I dunno. You don't think it's a bit . . . unusual?

Jasmine   I dunno. It's Big Meeting. I've been coming since I was little.

Abeni   So did your –

Jasmine   What?

Abeni   Nothing.

Jasmine   No, go on.

Abeni   I was gonna ask, did your dad ever come. Never mind.

Jasmine   I don't know. (*Pause.*) Why?

Abeni   It's just . . . it's very . . .

Jasmine   What?

Abeni   I just don't see a lot of brown people here.

Jasmine   OK. Does it matter?

Abeni   No. It doesn't. Ignore me. I'm just trying to process what I'm seeing.

Jasmine   Oh, come on. It's a parade and a party and, OK, it's a bit political, but it's just, you know. It's Big Meeting. Don't you have carnival in Manchester?

Abeni   That is not the same thing. (*Pause.*) You OK, Jaz?

Jasmine (*still subdued*)   Yeah.

Abeni   You sure?

Jasmine   Yeah. Actually, no. Cos now I'm sitting here looking for anyone who's not white.

Abeni   OK . . .

Jasmine   Cos this isn't just my corner of Durham. This is, like, from all over Durham. And there's definitely brown people living in Durham, but they're not here today.

Abeni   Well, this isn't exactly a scientific survey we're doing here . . .

Jasmine   I wish you'd never brought it up.

Abeni   Sorry, babes.

Pause. **Jasmine** *is annoyed.* **Abeni** *takes a couple of braids and shakes them to get her attention.*

Abeni   Jaz?

No response.

(*Cajoling.*) Jazzy . . .

Jasmine   Yeah.

Abeni   Sorry I ruined Big Meeting.

Jasmine   You didn't ruin Big Meeting.

Abeni   I did a bit though.

Jasmine   No. No, you didn't. It is what it is.

Abeni   You always felt a part of it. So you belong here. It's for you. Enjoy it.

Jasmine   Yeah. (*Standing.*) Come on.

Abeni   Where are we going?

Jasmine   Somewhere a bit quieter.

They exit.

Scene Eight

A little later that day. A wooded river bank in County Durham.

Abeni   Seriously, Jaz. Where are we going?

Jasmine   This'll do.

They sit, enjoy the sunshine. **Abeni** *checks her phone, puts it away again. A few moments of quiet.*

Abeni   No signal. What are we doing out here?

Jasmine   Getting a change of scenery. Enjoying the natural beauty of County Durham.

Abeni   Right.

Jasmine   Look at this. Blue skies! Trees, a nice river. Birds . . .

Abeni   You can get literally all those things in town. Plus actual toilets.

Jasmine   Yeah, but it's nice to do something different, you know? Something a bit more real.

Abeni   Nothing more real than getting murdered in the woods.

Jasmine (*laughing*)   Shut up! We're fine. *And* . . . I know my girl Abi. Here.

She reaches into her bag and pulls out a can of cider.

Abeni   You brought booze! You absolute star.

Jasmine   No problem.

She takes out a can for herself, opens it. They both drink quietly for a few moments.

Mam used to bring us out here. And Nana. (*Pause.*) We came with Dad once.

Abeni   You remember that?

Jasmine   Kind of. I found some photos Mam had stashed away. There's one of them looks like it's out here. I'm sat on a picnic blanket, wearing this dress with tomatoes on it, and you can see his legs. And when I looked at it, I could remember that day. Being here with him and Mam. We had strawberries.

Abeni   Whoa.

Jasmine   Yeah. (*Breezy.*) Anyway, it just made me remember this spot, and I thought . . . Might be a nice place to talk properly. So catch me up. How's work, how's home, how's life?

Abeni   Yeah. All good.

Jasmine   How's your mam?

Abeni   Good, yeah. Really good, actually. We've been spending a lot of time together.

Jasmine   I was thinking about her the other day.

Abeni   How come?

Jasmine   I read something about hair braiding. In South America, slaves used to braid maps into their hair to help them escape.

Abeni   Seriously? Is that true?

Jasmine   No idea. Quite cool if it is, though.

Abeni   Yeah. She would love that fact.

Jasmine   I kind of feel like I've been learning from her. All the stuff about braiding and that. Is that weird?

Abeni   Nah. She'd say that's how it's supposed to be. The community thing. Passing things on. (*African Mum voice.*) The sisterhood.

Jasmine (*laughs a little*)   I like that though.

Abeni   Me too. I like that I passed that on to you.

Pause. Slightly awkward.

Jasmine (*changing the subject*)   How was your trip back home?

Abeni   Oh! Really good, thanks. (*Unconvincing.*) Brilliant to see everyone.

Jasmine   Yeah?

Pause.

Abeni   Yeah. It was good, being with family. We talked about Dad a lot, which was sort of . . . bittersweet. Everyone's got their stories.

Jasmine   That's kind of lovely.

Abeni   Yeah, it was. I can't believe it's been two years. I still sometimes . . . Like, a few days ago, I turned on the TV and *Rocky* was on. And I literally turned to shout for Dad, cos he always liked to watch it 'live', as he put it. And then I remembered he's gone.

Jasmine   Abeni.

Abeni   Nah, it's OK. I kind of like that he's still there a bit, you know? Still in my life, in a way. (*Pause.*) So, yeah. The family stuff was a lot, but it was mostly good being back home. Different from what I expected, though. Being back on ends.

Jasmine Lots of changes?

Abeni No, not exactly. I mean, people have moved on, but it was more like . . . You know in a dream, when you're in a familiar place, and you know it is that place, but everything's a bit wrong? It was kind of like that.

Jasmine Like . . .?

Abeni Like I'd remembered it wrong. Threw me a bit. It's like, I've been *thinking* and *thinking* about going home and then I get there and it's something else.

Jasmine That's kind of sad.

Abeni (*shrugs*) I 'spose. I don't feel homesick any more. Just a bit, sort of, adrift. Like I'm waiting for someone to point me in the right direction. Anyway. How's things with your mum?

Jasmine No, it's fine. Pretty much back to normal. (*Pause.*) It's actually a bit shit.

Abeni What?

Jasmine Home. Mam. I don't know how to fix it. I need what I need, and I can't seem to get that without hurting her.

Abeni You're not. It's normal. You're leaving home, she's sad about it.

Jasmine It's a bit more than that. I've stirred up some other stuff. About me dad.

Abeni Oh. Shit.

Jasmine Yeah.

Abeni So . . . is he back in the picture or something?

Jasmine No, nothing like that. I just – you know me and Mam don't talk about the deep stuff. She's always hated us asking questions about Dad, and I didn't want to upset her, so I stopped asking. But I needed to know. So I asked, and she shut me down, and I got angry, and she got upset, and I got upset. But then she did tell us a bit.

Abeni   Like what?

Jasmine   His name, for a start.

Abeni   You didn't even know his name?

Jasmine   Well, no. I was just a bairn when he was around. He was 'Daddy'.

Abeni   Did you look him up?

Jasmine   Yeah. I found his Facebook. He's still in the North East. Married. Got a little girl. She looks about four. There's a really cute video of him doing her hair up in these little afro puffs.

Abeni   That's . . .

Jasmine   Yeah.

Abeni   Jaz. That's a lot.

Jasmine   It is. And it's not. I knew he must have a life, wherever he was. He wasn't just in limbo. But it's still . . . I still . . .

Abeni   Yeah.

Jasmine   Anyway.

Abeni   So what now?

Jasmine   Nothing.

Abeni   Seriously? You've got a little sister.

Jasmine   No. Not really. He's not been a dad to me, so . . . No. I wish I'd never looked. I didn't need to know that.

Abeni   Nah, come on. Look how much time and money people spend trying to find out who their great-great-great-great-grandad was. Everyone wants to know where they come from, and that's your *dad*. You need that.

Jasmine   But what about me Mam? It's still sitting there between us. It's a mess. What do I do?

Abeni   I don't know.

Jasmine (*sarcastic*)   Thanks, that's helpful.

Abeni   I don't have all the answers, Jaz. I don't even know what I'm doing myself right now. And I can't stop thinking that the best person to ask would be my dad.

Jasmine   Yeah. (*Pause*) Listen. I know I've been a bit of a shit mate . . .

Abeni *goes to say something and* **Jasmine** *gestures for her to stop*.

Jasmine   *Listen*. Having you here . . . It made such a difference. Like, I could see how to . . . That it was OK to . . . It wasn't just me . . . I don't know what I'm trying to say.

Abeni   S'alright. I get it.

Jasmine   Yeah. That's the difference. I don't have to explain everything. You just get it. And I don't know what you should be doing with life just now, but I think . . . if you're trying to work that stuff out, this isn't a bad place to stop for a bit.

Abeni   You really love it here, don't you?

Jasmine   Yeah. I do.

Abeni   So why'd you want to leave? Why not go to uni up here?

Jasmine   Cos. It doesn't always love me back.

Abeni   You can say that about the whole country.

Jasmine   True. But I want to meet more people like me. Like you.

Abeni   Only one of me, babes.

Jasmine (*laughing*)   Yeah. I'll have to get my fix when I'm back here for holidays.

Abeni   What makes you think I'm gonna be here? Maybe I wanna live abroad for a bit.

Jasmine   Me too! Italy. Or Spain.

Abeni   I was thinking America.

Jasmine   California! We'll go vegan and eat loads of fresh fruit and put avocados in everything.

Abeni   And learn to surf.

Jasmine   I don't actually like avocados.

Abeni   No one does, it's a con.

Jasmine   You'll work in a clothes shop and get us discounts.

Abeni   And you'll work in a cool bar and get us cheap drinks. And we'll never grow up.

Jasmine   And it'll be fun, even if it's a bit shit sometimes.

Abeni   We always have fun.

Jasmine   Yeah. We do.

Pause.

Abeni   Jaz . . . *What is that?*

Jasmine   What?

Abeni (*standing, pointing*)   *That*, there – massive – legs – is that a *heron?*

Jasmine (*also standing*)   Oh, yeah. It is, yeah.

Abeni (*quiet, slightly awed*)   Wow.

Jasmine   That's a lot of bird.

Abeni   That's amazing.

Jasmine   Yeah, I suppose it is. (*Looks at* **Abeni**.) Abi?

Abeni *is blinking a lot, trying not to cry.*

Jasmine   Abi, are you crying? Cos you saw a heron?

Abeni   I've had a drink, that's all.

Jasmine   It's OK if you are.

Abeni (*laughing at herself*)   I know. It's a *heron,* Jaz. I've never seen one before. It feels like a sign. I'm in the right place. I'm in the right place.

Jasmine   I mean . . . I'm pretty sure you can see a heron anywhere.

Abeni   But I didn't, did I? I saw one here.

End.

Cheer Up Slug

Tamsin Daisy Rees

Characters

Bean, *female. 16. A tin of golden syrup, Vimto, fairy lights and jam jars of slugs.*
Will, *male. Just turned 18. Hand sanitiser. A lot of it.*

Notes

/ indicates an interruption.

[ ] indicates words implied or meant to have said, but never are.

. . . indicates where a character is trailing off, or might have spoken, but doesn't.

Line breaks indicate pace of speech or character thought process.

Time passes is up to you.

Whey = Well.

CW   mention of sexual assault.

Thanks

This play would not have been written without the kindness and support of Zoe Cooper, Emily Collins, Ben Schwarz, Anna Ryder, Alison Scurfield and the Royal Court Writers Group North.

Thank you to everyone who has taken the time to read *Cheer Up Slug* in all it's stages, especially Louise Stephens, Jack Nicholls, Jane Fallowfield, Rebecca Tebbett, Dan Watson, Jill McAusland, Jackie Edwards, Luke Maddison, Lorne Campbell and Joe Douglas.

An empty field near a small village in County Durham. September.
Late afternoon.

Bean *enters with her small rucksack, wearing wellies and clutching*
her jars full of moss, seedlings and slugs. Whilst unpacking her
rucksack there should be a tin of golden syrup, a Moomin plastic
cup, a bottle of pink wine, Hobnobs, fig rolls, miniature shampoo.
Bean *quickly and efficiently puts up the tent.* **Will** *turns up*
abruptly. Analyses his surroundings.

Bean   Alright Will! /

Will   I'm not late /

Bean   I didn't say you – no, me grandad dropped us off on
his way to darts /

Will   You missed the induction briefing!

Will *notices his surroundings.*

I wanted to set this all up! When did you get here?

Bean   Oh, er I dunno actually. Maybe an hour / ago?

Will   Stupid bus /

Bean   You got the bus?

Will   Technically I was actually here before you though /

Bean   You never get the bus. Your mam doesn't like you
getting the bus.

Will   Not a big deal /

Bean   You should have said, we could have given you a lift!

Will *notices.*

Will   Dean's not here?

Bean   Uh, don't think, no /

Will   Are you shitting me! But he has to be here! Sixteen-
hundred hours, we had to be here, well, actually, we were
meant to be at the induction briefing at fifteen-hundred

hours but I was the only one taking this seriously enough to turn up, and Jake was very specifically clear we had to be here at sixteen-hundred hours Bean and it is, right now, fifteen-hundred and /

Bean   Why you talking weird?

Will   I'm not.

Bean   Yeh you are /

Will   Military time – doesn't matter – we're in the wilderness now, we have to take this seriously /

Bean (*laughing*)   It's hardly the wilderness /

Will (*pointing around*)   What's this then! What's this! (*Takes a jar.*) Wait, what is that /

Bean   My um my /

Will   Your what?

Bean   Slugs /

Will *disgusted, recoils and chucks it back.*

Will   You're proper weird sometimes.

Bean *silently takes the jar and cradles it.*

Bean   Hey, careful! My grandad gave me them.

Will   Why?!

Bean (*proudly*)   For the volunteering section in the activity log.

Will   Slugs?

Bean   Yeh well, you've been at the care home, and my grandad said I could just help him on the allotment. Anyway, these guys have been hanging around for ages. Didn't want to kill them or owt, cos that's a bit . . . but he still didn't want them on his geraniums, you know? We've been keeping them for a while. Hey, maybe it could be my skills section too! Like an experiment.

But like, a nice one.

I dunno. Anyway, grandad said it would be nice for them to get some fresh air. A little holiday! And he said these ones are definitely lucky /

Will   Slugs don't need holidays, Bean.

Beat.

Bean (*annoyed at being patronised*)   Yeh. I know. Just a joke.

Will (*frustrated*) I just –

I have volunteered every single Saturday morning for six months at the care home /

Bean   Thats great!

Will   And you . . . [just go piss about with your grandad!]

Bean   What?

Will   Nothing.

Beat. **Will** *is trying.*

That's really nice, Bean.

Pause. Gestures to what **Bean** *has brought.*

Will   So what have we got here then?

Bean *is confused.* **Will** *investigates.*

Will   This all you've brought!

Bean   What? I've got – there's my /

Will   Where's your survival bag?

Bean   My / what?

Will   Your whistle! Your sleeping bag /

Bean   Brought some blankets /

Will   But where's the food!

Bean   Got some Hobnobs and /

Will   Fuck's sake Bean.

Bean *is a bit gutted.*

Will   Shit. No. Sorry. I didn't mean.

Like. Great effort. Really. Good you tried. But it's not quite (*laughing*) what we're after /

Bean   Oh. OK. Just thought it'd be nice /

Will   No, no, not at all – like I say – great effort, just that you know. We actually need to be doing this properly.

So.

I'll start with the tent.

Bean   But I've already . . .

Will *ignores* **Bean** *and tries to 'fix' the tent.*

Bean   Will.

Will   Mmm?

Bean   Are you alright /

Will   How long's he gonna be?

Bean   Who?

Will   Who do you think, your boyfriend!

Bean   Oh. Yeh.

Uh.

Dunno? Give him a ring?

Will   What NO! ABSOLUTELY NOT, NO PHONES ALLOWED! ONLY FOR EMERGENCIES!

It says so in the leaflet!

Bean (*laughing*)   Jesus, sorry Will! Calm down.

Will   This is NOT FUNNY.

Pause.

I mean. Maybe we . . . could . . .

Bean   Just text him /

Will *snatches the phone.*

Will   No no no no no no no no! You know Jake is going to be checking on us! He could be anywhere!

At any moment!

Do you understand, Bean? Do you understand?

Bean   Why are you calling Mr Anderson Jake?

Will   What? I mean. (*Trying to be so cool and nonchalant.*) Well it's just . . . just his name, isn't it.

Bean   It's weird.

Pause.

Bean   You done something with your hair?

Will   No.

Bean   You've had a hair cut.

Will   What? Right. Oh. Yeh. Forgot.

Bean *inspects* **Will**'s *hair.*

Bean   Bit like /

Will   What? No /

Bean   Yeh with the (*Gestures.*)

Will   It's not like Dean's.

Beat.

Bean   I wasn't going to say it was like Dean's.

Will   Oh.

Bean   Looks nice.

Beat.

Will   Thanks.

Beat.

Will   Dean is coming, isn't he?

Bean *shrugs.*

Will   Cos if he's not we're buggered /

Bean   No we're not /

Will   We need the D of E /

Bean   I mean we don't *need* need it

Will   You might not but I do, and you know I do!

Bean   Do I?

Will   Yeh! So I can . . .

Do stuff.

Bean   Stuff?

Will   Yeh! Stuff!

Bean   What stuff?

Beat.

Will   Look just. He hasn't bailed, has he?

Bean   Maybe he was at football, so probably just be a bit late.

Be coming after football, won't he?

His sister'll be giving him a lift. She's, she's probably just late.

You know what that Fiat's like.

Will   Oh. Right.

Bean *starts eating Hobnobs.*

Will   I could have been really good at football too actually, if it wasn't for /

Bean (*mid mouthful of Hobnobs*)   Your orthopaedic insoles.

Will   I was going to say my studies.

But yeh.

I guess that too.

Bean   Not being funny but you were never properly into it though, were you?

Will   Actually Bean, I did that training course /

Bean   I don't think the after school club in year seven is a training course /

Will   Mr Thompson said I had what it takes /

Bean   Mr Thompson was a nonce!

Will   Is Dean coming or is he not coming?

Beat.

Bean   Course he is.

Will   Promise?

Bean   Yeh.

And like, if not he can just join us for the big walk tomorrow, yeh?

Will   What? No, no no no, he needs to do all of it, we all need to do all of it!

Bean   Yeh, alright! Am just saying, worst comes to worst, he can just join tomorrow then, yeh?

Beat.

Will   Yeh. Yeh alright.

But he is coming, isn't he?

Bean   Yeh!

Promise.

Just got to wait I guess.

There is a moment.

Will *carries on 'fixing' the tent,* **Bean** *starts eating sweets.*

Bean   Here, have one of these, Will /

Will   No /

Bean   Honestly, have one /

Will   No man /

Bean   No go on, they're dead good. Brought them specially /

Will   Will you stop distracting me!

Beat. **Bean** *looks a little crestfallen.*

Will   Ah shit.

Look. Bean. I'm [sorry]. Didn't mean to [snap].

Beat.

Alright, go on then. Pass us one.

Bean *perks up and rushes back over with a fistful of sweeties. Bit embarrassed, she starts making daisy chains.*

Will   Bean.

Bean   Mmm?

Will (*examining them*)   Why are they in the shape of eyeballs?

Bean   They're from last Halloween! Saved them up specially! Apart from the ghost marshmallows, always eat them in one go /

Will   It's – there's no way we can eat this!

Bean   It's just some chocolate /

Will   We'll get diarrhoea! /

Bean   Chocolate never / goes off

Will   That's just not true /

Bean   What me grandad told me /

Will   Well, he's wrong /

Bean   No he isn't!

Will   We'll get the shits! /

Bean   We won't, man, don't be daft /

Will   Well, I didn't bring any Imodium /

Bean   Will, you're being ridiculous, pass them back then /

Will (*stands up and moves away with them*)   I'm chucking them out /

Bean (*they start to wrestle*)   ARE YOU BOLLOCKS I've been saving them for months /

Will   I'm not going to let you give yourself the shits /

Bean   WHY DO YOU CARE IF I GET THE SHITS.

They're stuck in their wrestling position.

There is a moment.

They rearrange themselves quite hurriedly.

Bean   Will. Uh.

Mam.

She told me, about your parents and /

Will   Fuck's sake.

Bean   I didn't want to not, but I thought you should know that I / [know]

Will   Why?

Why, why why why would she do that?

Pause.

Bean   Well. Just thought.

Going to have a nice time, now though like, aren't we!

Beat.

Nice here, isn't it?

It's my favourite.

Pause. **Bean** *is enjoying the environment.* **Will** *is anxiously trying to rearrange the tent.*

Bean   Hey, Will.

Guess what I've got.

Will.

Will.

Will.

Will.

Will.

Will /

Will   What, man!

Bean   Want some pink wine?

Will   Where you get that from!

Bean   Nicked it from Mam, didn't I /

Will   No no no no no no no no, Bean, no man! We'll get disqualified!

Bean   No we won't /

Will   They're watching!

Bean   Who's watching?

Will   Jake is coming to check on us, they said, at the induction briefing!

Bean   Mr Anderson is not going to turn up, he'll be getting pissed with Miss Daniels and the other leaders.

Come on.

Come onnnnnnnnn! Don't be boring! It's fun!

Beat.

Will   Don't even like wine /

Bean   Me neither! But it's OK. I brought some fizzy Vimto too, and then it tastes just like pop!

Will   Height of sophistication.

Bean   Exactly!

Will   Haven't even got a glass /

Bean   I've got my Moomin cup.

You could use it, you know. If you like?

A moment. And then **Will** *gives in. They awkwardly arrange themselves just outside their tent den.* **Will** *takes a while hand sanitising and arranging himself, obviously uncomfortable.* **Bean** *pours wine into her Moomin cup for* **Will** *and tops it up with Vimto.* **Bean** *realises she hasn't got another cup, so alternates between swigging from the bottle of wine and swigging from the can of Vimto. A moment.* **Bean** *opens up a tin of golden syrup and eats a spoonful.* **Will** *checks his watch.*

Will   You do realise, if one of us doesn't turn up we'll get disqualified. We need a minimum of three people, Bean, now this is, this is, this is actually getting quite serious, because if Jake comes back to check on us he'll see there's only the two of us and then . . . we won't be able to do it properly and then . . . we won't get it /

Bean   Get what?

Will   The D of E! Duke of Edinburgh! The award!

Bean   So?

Will   So! So! So we won't have it, we won't be able to, able to /

Bean   But it doesn't matter, Will? Can't we just /

Will   Why you even doing this if you're not going to take it seriously!

Bean   Why you even doing this when you obviously hate it!

Pause.

They drink.

Bean *has another spoonful of golden syrup.*

Will   I don't hate it.

Beat.

I just. I need this. For uni. I need the best possible chance to get in. I've made a spreadsheet, listed with my grades crossed with my extra curricular activities and I need . . . an edge.

Bean   And your Duke of Edinburgh bronze practice expedition, is your edge?

I thought you were doing that progression thing with Durham Uni? So you don't have to worry about an edge, they'll sort it all out for you?

Pause.

Will (*tentatively*)   I. I think . . .

I think . . . I want to go to Brighton.

Beat.

Like for uni and that.

Bean   Oh. Right. Seaside's nice!

Will   I think it'd be good. You know? Yeh, by the seaside. Properly cultural like, with all the you know, music and clubs /

Bean   You?!

Will   Whey, why not!

Bean   Sorry, no just. Sorry /

Will   Bit different. I'd like to try it anyway.

Bean   What do you want to learn?

Will   History? Or maybe like you know like maybe even Film studies . . . or or something you know. Cultured. Proper you know. Like. Learning about . . . [stuff].

Bean   Right.

Beat.

Will   Mam wants us to go to Durham though, 'cause it'll be cheaper if I live at home but.

Think she just doesn't like being on her own now me dad's [left].

But I just. Honestly like.

I couldn't. Went to the open day. And I just hated it. All these lecturers and these professors – proper smug.

The whole time, I were just thinking: I know this place better than any of you. I do. I know every single bus route into town and where they'll break down and where the drivers always stop for a tab.

I know the quickest way across town when it's the miners' gala. Remember that year I was playing in the band /

Bean   Oh yeh! Was nice you playing the cornet, wasn't it?

Will   And we were waiting for our turn.

Bean   Do you still play it?

Will   And it was proper pissing down.

Bean   I was there! Remember? I made a banner!

Will   And I look up, we were past Elvet Bridge, you know, down near the courts.

Bean   You've told me this story.

Will   And I look up. And there's these proper rahs, just laughing out the window. Laughing! Durham Uni.

Bean   Not everyone there would be like that /

Will (*as if talking to the rahs*)   I know this place better than all of you. And you're here – making ME feel unwelcome?

Beat.

It's like everyone's forgotten. Like on the telly when they talk about the North: there's Yorkshire. Then there's Scotland. Whey – where the bloody hell do we fit?!

A moment.

Bean   Why do you want to leave if you like it here so much?

Beat.

Will   I don't like it.

Bean   Why you care what them professors think, then /

Will   I don't /

Bean   You do /

Will   Just . . .

Bean   ???

Beat.

Will   Just what you do, isn't it. Move on.

Weak to stay where you're from, isn't it?

Beat.

Bean   Is it?

Beat.

Will   What about you?

Bean?

Bean, what are you going to do?

Bean   Dunno.

Will   Come on, you must have an idea.

Bean *shrugs*.

Bean   Not really.

Will   Come on, Bean. You're sixteen. You must have a drive.

Bean   A what?

Will   A, a, a thing!

Bean *thinks*.

Bean   I like being outside.

Will   Yeh, well, that's not like a thing though, is it.

Bean   Why not?

Will   What about college? You could do health and social! Hey, you could do your placement at the care home! I could help with that, you know.

Beat. Another spoonful of golden syrup.

Bean   I dunno.

I spend ages, just like Googling stuff. Places in the world I might like to go to, or search for jobs and stuff I could do. Like sometimes I imagine being in one of those offices with like those big glass doors, and I can wear matching suits, with the big shoulders. And I'd wear loads and loads and loads of lipstick.

Bean *starts putting on lipstick*.

It's a bit sticky and a mess with the golden syrup.

Loads of it.

Just everywhere.

Bean *starts putting lipstick on* **Will**. **Will**, *surprisingly, lets her.*

Bean   But I dunno cos. Don't think it's really me.

I do like it here.

It's not that I don't.

It's just that.

Just not all the time. You know?

The people. Not always . . . but, they can be . . .

There is a moment.

Bean *snaps out of it, drinks, and places out her jars carefully.*

Bean *gives* **Will** *a cloth.*

Bean (*forced*)   This'll be nice though! All of us together again.

Will *furiously rubs at his face.*

Will   This, this, this is ridiculous.

There's two of us! This is not an expedition team /

Bean (*checks watch*)   Not been that long. It doesn't matter /

Will   It's embarrassing!

Bean *takes another spoonful of golden syrup.*

Pause.

Bean   Do you want to . . . do you want to play a game then? While we're waiting?

Will   A game?

Bean   Yeh! It'll be fun!

Will   What's the point if there's just two of us?

Bean   So /

Will   Jesus. Have you ever seen anything more sad than only two people doing a D of E expedition?

Bean   Stop being such a tit, man /

Will   I'm not being /

Bean   You are, you're being smelly bum /

Will   Wow, 'smelly bum', really mature /

Bean   Smelly bum bum /

Will   You're actually just being very / childish

Bean   Alright Sluggy /

Will   Sluggy! Jesus Christ. Haven't heard that one in a while.

Bean (*threatening with her jars*)   Sluggy's scared of slugs!

Will   No I'm not /

Bean   Sluggy's scared of slugs! Sluggy's scared of slugs!

Will   Stop it /

Bean   Sluggy's scared of / slugs!

Will   That's it!

Will *starts to try to chase* **Bean**. **Bean** *manages to get away, vaguely threatening him with her tin of golden syrup, but they end up wrestling, laughing. It is not particularly flirtatious or sexual, more like a brother and sister wrestling.*

Will *suddenly stops.*

Will   You are such a child.

Bean *is red faced and out of puff.*

Bean   No I'm not.

They sit down next to each other again. Bit awkward.

Bean *has another spoonful.*

Bean   Haven't hung out like this – just us two I mean, like in ages /

Will   Yeh, well. Since you got with me best mate. Not really had time, have you /

Bean   You've been busy too! Like with . . . stuff.

Guess it's just. Bit weird not seeing you everyday /

Will   Yeh, whey we're not kids anymore, are we?

Beat.

Will   / Why did you get with Dean? He's not even your type

Bean   / Shall we play the game then?

Beat.

Bean   My type?

Will   Yeh, I just mean /

Bean   Not even what?

Will   Just that. Well, he's more . . . football than Attenborough / you know?

Bean   How would you know / what my type is

Will   Come on, we've known each other, what, eight years?

Bean   Nine.

No, ten.

No, nine.

Nine. Yeh, nine, cos we moved from Paragon Street to next door so /

Will   Am just saying, I know you pretty well? Like maybe even more than you know yourself /

Bean   OK /

Will   Not that I'm saying I know more about you than you do, I'm not saying, that's not what I'm saying, like, at all! Just that I do know you better than maybe you know yourself.

Beat.

Bean   Right.

Pause.

Some time passes. Maybe they are in a weird position, **Will** *inspecting* **Bean**'s *face. It's not sexual or flirtatious.*

Will   How come you don't really wear make up?

Bean   What?

Will   Like, rest of the lasses at school – all eyebrows and, and mascara pens and that.

Bean   I dunno. Don't really like the feeling I guess.

Beat.

Will   Is it cos of when we were in Mrs Green's class?

Bean   Eh?

Will   You remember? Year 4?

That one lunchtime we were playing.

Jessica Nicholson had brought in that that that box of make up stuff, but it were just proper naff like free stuff from magazines /

Bean   Sabrina's Secrets!

Will   Eh?

Bean   Sabrina the Teenage Witch! That was the make up!

Will   Right, whatever. So do you remember /

Bean   (*remembers*)   Oh my god, yeh /

Will   Yeh, right! I did your make up for you!

Bean   What?

Will   Yeh in the yard at dinner, we'd always go to that bit of wall near that tree, remember?

Bean   Yeh, I remember /

Will   And then you got jealous of everyone being around Jessica and you wanted to join in, so I nicked loads of the stuff for you /

Bean   I didn't get jealous /

Will   And and and and then you – bless you, Bean, honestly – you were so scared (*Laughing.*) of how to put it on properly? Do you remember?

Bean   No one had shown me before /

Will   Yeh, so you got me to!

Bean   No, Will.

Will   Eh?

Bean   That's not what happened.

Will   Yeh it is /

Bean   It's not, why are you /

Will   I'm not lying /

Bean   You made me put Jessica's make up on you!

Will   That's not /

Bean   Yeh it is! You asked me to do your make up so I did /

Will   What? That's not /

Bean   You wanted the . . . the glitter stuff for eyes. And that really sticky lipgloss. Oh and that blue nail varnish! I painted your nails / remember

Will   What the fuck are you on about /

Bean   What?

No it was.

It was nice, Will.

It was really lovely.

Beat.

We were just playing.

Beat.

I should have played with those girls, they'd have shown me.

I'm just.

Not much of a join-er in-er, I guess.

Beat.

Will   They were complete bitches.

Bean   No they weren't /

Will   Yeh they were /

Bean   Just cos Jessica didn't fancy you /

Will   What! No that's, no – that's just – ridiculous, they were all just really – cliquey – and /

Bean   They were nine, Will.

Beat.

Some times passes.

Bean   Do you want to play another game?

Will   Could play truth or dare?

Bean   Would you rather have a willy for a nose or willy fingers?

Will   What? That's not truth or dare /

Bean   Would you rather be . . . fingered by a sloth or give up kisses for the rest of your life?

Will   You're not playing it properly / You are such a child.

Bean   What?

Will   I dare you to take your top off.

Pause.

Bean   What?

Beat.

Will   Shit sorry! Wasn't thinking!

Course.

Don't do that.

That's

That's silly.

Bean   Right.

Will   It was a joke – I was joking.

Beat.

Bean   I don't get it?

Will   Yeh, well, you wouldn't.

Beat.

Some time passes.

Will   I'm learning guitar, actually.

Bean   Are you?

Will   Well.

I'm going to.

Me and Dean.

Gonna join his band.

Probably.

Bean   That's cool.

Will   Yeh, yeh it is actually.

Some time passes.

Bean   How can you tell if someone fancies you?

How can you tell if you fancy them?

Will   I dunno.

You just like their smile?

There's something in their laugh; or you just. Do.

You know if you know. You know?

Bean   I don't think so.

Pause.

Some time passes.

Maybe there's a long moment where you can see **Will** *trying to set up the trangia and organise all the tent items, while* **Bean** *is playing and organising her slugs and jars of moss.*

Then –

Will   Remember? Do you remember /

Bean   We were five and /

Will   No we weren't, man /

Bean   No, we were, we were five, and the side of the school /

Will   The, the side of the school, we kept painting the wood /

Bean   But with water so it wouldn't /

Will   Yeh exactly, with water, so wouldn't, so it / it kept evaporating

Bean   Kept evaporating!

Will   Wouldn't dry! All day we'd paint again and again and again /

Bean   No one even told us /

Will   Remember Dean?

Used to mow down those grass houses we made for the bees on his scooter /

Bean   Did he?

Will   Yeh, when you were seven, remember?

Bean   Seven?

Will   Maybe eight?

Anyway, yeh, bloody tinker with his scooter, nearly got the bees n'all /

Bean   I don't remember the /

Will   Yeh, you do man, the, there was that time we found that, that bumblebee – remember! That bumblebee we found at dinner and, and it wasn't well so you tried to make us all save it /

Bean   Mrs Fuzzybottom!

Will   Yeh, Mrs Fuzzybottom!

And you were dead upset, you didn't cry though, you just had such a serious face, honestly, proper dead stone cold.

And just kept demanding we get sugar water, like we, like we were in a hospital and you were the nurse, everyone flapping /

Bean   But you didn't /

Will   Nah, I didn't /

Bean   You got some Ribena /

Will I got some Ribena. Had to swap two Pokémon stickers for it /

Bean And you were dead chuffed with yourself /

Will Whey, I was, wasn't I, saved the day /

Bean What you talking about?

Will Eh? Saved the, uh, the day, didn't I?

Beat.

What with the Ribena and that.

Beat.

That's what you're meant to do, isn't it?

Bean You thick? Course you don't give pissing Ribena to a bumblebee /

Will Whey, how was I supposed to know!

Bean You didn't save it! You didn't even try!

Will Eh /

Bean You drowned Mrs Fuzzybottom /

Will Nah, no, I didn't /

Bean How can you not remember?

Beat.

Bean You drowned Mrs Fuzzybottom cos it made Jessica laugh. Then you mowed down the grass house I'd made. On Dean's scooter.

Beat.

That was you. Were never Dean. He didn't do that.

Pause.

They both resume their activities, playing with slug jars and organising their equipment.

Some time passes.

Eventually –

Bean   I just think, maybe, you should lighten up a bit.

Will   Excuse me?

Oh, like Dean, is it?

Bean   I'm not saying that.

Will   Is though, isn't it. Cos he's all . . . spontaneous and that.

Bean   Uh. I guess?

Will   And he's fine with all your slugs and that?

Bean   Shall we just play something else?

Will   What's the point?

Beat.

Bean   Uh.

Well. We could . . .

We could . . .

We could do those challenges, you have to do anyway, for the award? Like, as a team bonding?

Will   Just the two of us?

Bean   Yeh!

Will   Bean. I don't think we need to bond /

Bean   Yeh, I know, but like. You wanted to do it properly. So.

Will   OK.

Bean   So. Let's. OK. Um /

Will   Bean /

Bean   I challenge you to eat all of these fig rolls!

Will *stares at her in disbelief. Then laughs and takes a couple.*
Bean *sort of laughs in relief.*

Will   My turn /

Bean   You haven't eaten all the fig rolls.

Will   I'm not going to eat all the fig rolls.

Bean   But you have to! Do it properly!

Will   Don't be stupid /

Bean   Alright, another challenge! Do a . . . do a cartwheel!

Will   What!

Bean   Hand stand!

Will *starts laughing.*

Bean   Forward roll, come on!

*They both start doing cartwheels/forward rolls/hand stands. They
end up slumped, giggling and silly and giddy, out of breath and in a
pile on the floor.* **Will** *might start to hand sanitise.*

Will   OK. Your challenge is . . . to . . . to take your wellies off!

Bean *isn't fussed by it.*

Will   And, and, and your socks!

Bean *doesn't react.*

Will   And to run around in the mud!

Bean *looks a little bemused but shrugs and skips around.*

Will   Fuck! I thought you wouldn't want to get, you know
dirty.

Not like that!

They both blush a bit.

Bean   OK, my turn!

Take your wellies off!

Will   NO WAY /

Bean   I did /

Will   Yeh, but you're /

Bean   I'm what?

Will   You know . . .

Beat.

Will   Oh fuck it, fine!

Will, *grimacing, takes off his wellies.*

Bean   And now your socks /

Will   NO WAY, NOT THE SOCKS /

Bean   You are not taking this seriously enough, Sluggy /

Will   Fuck off, fine!

Very delicately, **Will** *takes off his socks and squelches in the mud tentatively.*

Bean   Quite nice, isn't it?

Will   I would not call this nice.

Bean *pushes* **Will** *a bit.*

Will   What you playing at!

Will *shoves* **Bean** *back.* **Bean** *is giggling, crouches down and puts mud on her face.*

Will   Oh my god, this is mental /

Bean   Have a go!

Will   I cannot!

Bean   Yeh you can!

Over the next few lines **Bean** *is trying to attack* **Will** *with mud and* **Will** *is trying to defend himself.* **Bean** *chases* **Will**.

Will   No way, am not having any of this /

Bean   Come on, Will, part of the wilderness now /

Will   Are we bollocks /

Bean   Got to camouflage yourself /

Will   No bloody way /

Bean   Survival, innit /

Will   Absolutely not /

Bean   I'll do it for you /

Will   NO YOU WON'T! Get over here /

Bean   Eyy, Sluggy's joining in!

Will *arms himself with the golden syrup, and chases* **Bean** *instead.* **Bean** *is giggling hysterically now.*

Will   Come on, have some lovely golden syrup /

Bean   No flipping way!

Will   Delicious golden syrup /

Bean   Piss off /

Will   (*resisting the urge to hand sanitise*)   Lovely and . . . sticky!

Bean   You're crackers!

They end up stuck in a sort of wrestling position and stare each other out for a few moments, waiting for the other to make a move.

Bean *swipes at his face with some mud (gently).*

Will *gasps in shock, then starts laughing and pours the golden syrup onto his head.*

Bean   Oh my god!

Will *is still laughing.*

Bean   Will, what the /

Will   I'm just a, uh, a mad bastard!

Bean *is shocked and giggling. She goes over and touches his hair.*

Bean   So sticky!

Will   Uh. Yeh.

Will *is coming a bit more down to earth now and looks uncomfortable.*

Will   I've got some baby wipes, in my . . . Do you mind?

Bean   What? Oh yeh, I'll.

Bean *goes rummaging inside the tent.* **Will** *tentatively sits down, hands poised so as not to touch the golden syrup or the mud.*

Bean's *phone pings.*

Will   We're not meant to have phones!

Only in emergencies!

Only in ABSOLUTE emergencies!

Bean (*off*)   You say something?

Will   Your phone /

Bean (*off*)   What?

Will   You've got a (*Glances at phone.*) It's Dean!

Bean (*off*)   Can't hear you /

Will   You got a text off Dean!

Bean (*off*)   Can't find these wipes

Will *leans over to read the text properly.*

Bean *come back out of the tent holding the baby wipes.*

Bean   Bingo! Never would have thought to bring /

Will   Your boyfriend text.

Will *chucks the phone to* **Bean**.

Bean *reads the phone. Is shocked. Drops the phone back onto the ground.*

Bean   Right.

Will *ignores her.*

Bean   Did you read it?

Beat.

Not, not very nice, is it?

Will *ignores her.*

Bean   Are you OK?

Will   You really piss me off sometimes.

Bean *is a bit stunned.*

Bean   I don't understand /

Will   Yeh well you wouldn't would you!

Why's he calling you a-a-a

How's that even possible, that's an oxymoron –

WHY IS HE SAYING THOSE THINGS ABOUT YOU?

Beat.

Bean   Why are you – I mean, I should be /

Will   Well, 'cause, 'cause, 'cause now . . . there's no way we can complete the expedition!

Beat.

Bean   What?

Will   If your boyfriend is calling you – that! He's not going to turn up is he!

Bean   That's why you're angry?

Because you don't think we can do the expedition?

Will   I just think if we are going to remain, you know . . . professional /

Bean   Your best mate called me /

Will   What? No I mean.

Obviously that's. Not on.

But. (*Clears throat.*)

Just that the expedition.

Comes first, doesn't it.

Bean *is a bit tearful and nods.*

Bean   Got to. Wash my face and stuff.

Will   Cool.

Bean *makes to leave.*

Will   I mean.

Just a joke though, isn't it?

Just banter, like.

Isn't it?

Beat.

Bean   Course.

Just a laugh.

A small moment. Time passes.

Bean *and* **Will** *are now just outside the tent. It is darker now, and colder.* **Bean**'s *tent decorations are looking shabby but sweet with fairy lights glowing a bit.* **Will** *is sat crossed legged on a cushion with his back to* **Bean.** **Bean** *is kneeling behind him, trying to pick out the golden syrup with a small comb and a pair of scissors.*

Will   OW!

Bean   Shit / sorry

Will   It's fine / sorry

Bean   Sorry /

Will   Don't apologise / you're doing me a favour

Bean   Shit yeh sorry / Oh fuck

Will *laughs then cries in pain as* **Bean** *accidentally pulls his hair again.*

Bean   Oh god!

Will   No-no I'm sorry it's fine /

Bean   Still / though

Will   No, no, really, please just get it OW / FUCK

Bean   Shit /

Will   Shall we have a break?

Bean   I'm nearly /

Will   Let's have a break.

Will *turns round to face her. They're both a bit embarrassed.*

Will *is staring at* **Bean** *a bit too long.*

Bean *sort of stares back confused.*

Will *suddenly looks away embarrassed.*

Bean   Will? What you doing?

Will (*shakes out of it*)   Sorry!

Bean   You alright /

Will (*clears throat*)   What? Yeh, just the. Sorry – the uh, the lights just /

Bean   Oh they're quite /

Will   Bright, yeh /

Bean   I was gonna say just a bit.

Crap really.

Will   Crap?

Bean   Yeh, I figured you wouldn't /

Will   I wouldn't what?

Bean   Well. Like them. Cause they're not like you know on the list of proper stuff /

Will   I think they're lovely.

Beat.

Bean   Oh.

Beat.

Good.

There is a moment.

Will (*clears throat*)   I mean, it is quite funny how unprepared you are /

Bean   I'm not / unprepared

Will   Aw, Beanie it's fine, I'm not mad at you or anything /

Bean   Mad?

Will   Yeh cause, you know, I'm the – you know /

Bean   The what?

Will   Not that I'm in charge, I'm not saying that, just that you know /

Bean   What are you trying to say, Will?

Will   Nothing! Just that you aren't really the . . . camping type.

Beat. **Bean** *glowers at him.*

Bean   I brought the fucking tent.

Will   Yeh – OK – fair play, you did, in fairness bring the tent, but also (*Laughing, gestures to the decorations.*) all of this /

Bean   I thought it'd be nice?

Will   Yeah exactly! It's just really funny /

Bean   Funny?

Will   No, not, not funny, just like, you know. Endearing.

Bean   I've been camping before /

Will   Yeh but /

Bean   I grew up here before we moved /

Will   Whey aye, I know that /

Bean   So I know this place better than you!

Will   So I figured you'd be more prepared!

Bean   I'm not the one scared of the countryside.

Will   Woah woah woah, hey now, hey I'm not – it's not that I'm *scared*, it's just, I just . . . don't like it.

Beat.

Bean   I love it, me.

Like everything about it. The moors. The heather. The sheep.

Beat.

I even like the moss.

Will   Moss?!

Bean   Well. Yeh. It just feels nice really doesn't it.

Springy.

Beat. **Bean** *goes back to combing* **Will***'s hair a bit.*

Used to have to walk down the back lane to school, with my Grandad. He'd walk with us. Make sure I got there OK . . .

we'd always be late, and I'd be so scared I'd get in trouble I'd almost wet myself. But he kept stopping along the way and make me look at different stuff – funny stones or plants or the way the pavement cracked together and how to walk around the broken glass.

And moss.

He'd find the moss on the highest walls and pick me up under my armpits and shove my face in it and make me pat it.

And now. Well. Just. It's.

Beat.

Just nice really. Springy.

Beat.

Will   Yeh. Springy.

Beat.

You don't half come out with some rubbish.

Bean *is a bit crushed.*

Bean *looks up.*

Bean   Stars are nice /

Will   It's cloudy as fuck /

Bean   My grandad told me dying stars look like thoughts. No I mean – that's not right – like. Shit. Like. Like forming thoughts. That's right. Growing thoughts.

Do you see what I mean? Do you understand /

Will   Bean, what are you /

Bean   OK, OK! It's just that like. OK. Ah bollocks . . . like. In your brain.

Look. He told me . . . there are more connections in your mind than there are galaxies in the universe.

So there are more universes in your head when you're born.
And then they are pruned the more you grow.

But – but it's OK. Like. It's essential that they're pruned.
They have to be.

Beat.

And I quite like that idea? You know? The different
universes in your head have to be pruned. Some bits that
you don't want in your head anymore. Those bits. Those
universes HAVE to be pruned /

Will   I don't think it actually works like that /

Bean   No – no it does! It does! All the horrible things can
just be pruned . . .

Bean *is playing with the scissors.*

Bean   Just snip snip snip /

Will   Bean, stop it /

Bean   Snip snip /

Will   Bean /

Bean   Isn't that great! All the bits you really don't need in
your brain anymore don't have to be there! Because it's
ESSENTIAL they're gone /

Will   Stop it /

Bean   But do you understand, do you get it /

Will   Of course I fucking do.

Pause.

Bean   I didn't mean about your parents. That's not what I.

Beat.

Bean   Will /

Will   Just shut up.

Pause.

Will   Ring Dean. Get him to come.

Beat.

Bean   But you said, the phones /

Will   Fuck's sake – this, this – THIS is actually an emergency now, so.

Ring him.

Bean *doesn't react.*

Will   He's been telling all the lads, you know.

That you can't get enough.

Bean *is stunned.*

Will   Tell him you're here, ready and waiting for him.

Bean *doesn't react.*

Will   Tell him you're gagging for it.

Bean *doesn't react.*

Will   Tell him you're literally gagging to gag on his / cock

Bean   We broke up.

Beat.

Will   Eh?

Bean   I text him.

Beat.

Will   You!

Bean *nods.*

Will   Why didn't you say?

Bean *shrugs.*

Will   When?

Bean   Yesterday.

Beat.

Will   What?

Yesterday?

You dumped Dean, yesterday?

Via text?

And you thought he'd still come?

Bean   I just thought /

Will   Are you a fucking idiot?

Bean (*frighteningly aggressive yet quiet*)   Shut up.

Huge, deafening pause.

Bean   Last week. Went to his for the first time.

Beat.

We had sex?

Will   You [fucked]! You actually /

Bean   No! We – I /

Will   You fucking slut.

Pause.

Bean   It hurt, Will.

It really, really hurt.

Beat.

He [fucked me]. And I couldn't.

I tried to leave. But.

Beat.

I just froze, Will.

I froze.

I just lay there.

Bean *maybe is crying but maybe smiling at the same time.*

As though in disbelief that this horrible horrible violence has happened to her.

And he kept [fucking me].

Beat.

His room was minging.

You'd have hated it! Kept thinking how he should do a proper hoover and get some Febreze.

Lynx. And PE kit smell.

Bobbly sheets.

Had crumbs in it too.

Stale crusts, pizza and stuff.

Beat.

It wasn't me.

None of it. He. He didn't see, me.

I wasn't anyone.

Beat.

I just [cried].

Watching his stupid light up alarm clock.

Waiting.

Beat.

And after a while, he stopped. After a while.

Beat.

After a while.

Maybe **Will** *reaches over and holds her fingers.*

There is a moment.

Bean   He went downstairs to his mam's kitchen – she was out, course, so was his nan.

And he made me some toast.

Used proper butter and I hated it. Dead salty.

Only have margarine at home, or Nordpak for Grandad.

But this butter.

It wouldn't melt properly so all the lumps were just sitting, on the top.

Got caught in my throat, and I couldn't [swallow].

He didn't have any of toast, of course.

Always took pride in pointing out how his thigh gap was bigger than mine.

Beat.

Gave me a glass of orange juice. And said it was OK. That it was OK.

Beat.

Toast.

And orange juice.

Isn't that a weird thing to do?

Will *doesn't react.*

Bean   Isn't that a really weird thing to do, Will?

Will *doesn't react.*

Bean   Isn't that a really FUCKING WEIRD THING TO DO.

Beat.

I hate orange juice.

Beat.

It had bits in it too. Absolutely rank.

There is a moment.

Bean *blinks and sort of remembers where she is.*

I walked home.

Beat

And I just.

I dunno how.

Autopilot.

Kept having to check.

Behind my shoulders.

Like someone was following me.

(*Laughs.*) Like someone could just [attack me].

Beat.

Kept flick-flicking my head around.

Darting.

Checking.

Beat.

My –

Chest –

Bean *puts hand to her chest.*

There might be music or a sound, something unbearable.

Or perhaps the silence is unbearable.

It's like I'm in the swimming pool, under water. My ears all, all fuzzy.

And.

That. Song.

That stupid song.

It gets louder and louder and louder and louder and louder until everyone is uncomfortable. Maybe **Bean** *even dances a little.*

Going round and round and round and round and I cannot.

That stupid song.

That stupid song he played on his iPhone.

That stupid song he played on his stupid fucking iPhone while he [FUCKED ME].

THAT STUPID FUCKING SONG

Stops abruptly.

A moment.

Text him later.

Saying I feel a bit ill and that.

Bit weird. Ask if I can ring?

Doesn't reply.

Says he can't, he's busy.

Playing FIFA.

Beat.

I do a sick, actually. Isn't that weird?

And I go sit in the bath.

Beat.

Water's dead hot though.

Beat.

I don't notice till I'm out and it's proper red all down my legs.

(*Gently laughing.*) Had to have Sudocrem under me clothes all week!

Beat.

Still hurts, actually.

Huge pause.

Will   Fuck.

Beat.

So now.

I guess we. Uh.

Will *arranges himself a bit awkwardly.*

Bean *is sort of ignoring him in a bit of a daze.*

Will   Do you want. Uh.

If we just.

Shall we /

Bean   . . . ?

Will   Just /

Bean   What?

Will   Just – you know.

What with.

So like. Now I guess. We'll just.

We'll . . .

I suppose.

Will *grabs* **Bean** *and kisses her.* **Bean** *does not kiss back, and in no way has shown physical affection towards* **Will** *before during or after. It is a shock. After some moments* **Bean** *physically recoils and* *stands up. Another option is that* **Will** *attempts to kiss* **Bean**, *and* **Bean** *recoils.*

Bean   WHAT THE FUCK /

Will *is shocked at her reaction.*

Bean   WHAT ARE YOU PLAYING AT /

Will   Eh?!

Bean *rubs her mouth furiously.*

Will   I thought you wanted /me to

Bean   Why would you think that!

Will   Thought it'd . . .

Bean   . . . ?

Will   . . . help?

Bean   Help?

Beat.

Bean   . . . help?!

Will   Oh fuck /

Bean   Fucking hell /

Will   Fuck fuck fuck /

Bean (*struggling, bit teary but angry teary not sad*)   You . . . dick /

Will   I just figured cos /

Bean   Cos what /

Will   Whey, cos after Dean being a bit. You know.

Bean *turns and glowers at* **Will**.

Bean   A bit?

Will   . . . a bit shit.

Bean   'A bit shit'.

Will   What?

Bean   Pack it in /

Will   I don't even care that Dean said you were shit, I can teach . . .

Bean *glowers at* **Will**.

Pause.

Bean   You're not a friend at all.

Beat.

You're actually really awful, aren't you?

Will *is a bit stunned.*

Bean *makes to go.* **Will** *suddenly comes back down to earth, hurriedly looks around and calls after* **Bean**.

Will   BEAN. BEAN. BEAN THAT-THAT SHIT YOU SAID ABOUT THE STARS AND THAT. ALL THE MOSS. JUST LIKE. SO YOU KNOW.

(*Hurriedly.*) IT'S NOT DEEP AND IT'S NOT CLEVER IT'S JUST SHIT.

Bean *turns to look back at* **Will**.

Bean *goes to leave.*

Will   What are you doing?

Bean *starts packing.*

Will   You can't.

Jake's coming to check up on us in the morning, OK. We have the big walk tomorrow!

Bean *ignores him and continues.*

Will   We can't leave, we'll get disqualified, we'll get bollocked we'll get –

Bean *ignores him and continues.*

Will   What – what about your grandad!

Bean *stops.*

Will   Can you imagine?

Teaching you about all of . . . this. Then you getting disqualified?

Beat.

For fuck's sake, it's raining, Bean. You can't go out in this.

Just need to last until morning. OK? And then we can do the hike.

Just the morning.

Can you do that?

Bean?

Can you do that?

Bean?

Bean?

BEAN

BEAN CAN YOU FUCKING DO THAT?

Bean *stops. Doesn't look at* **Will**.

Pause.

Bean *starts unpacking, slowly.*

Will   Good.

Good, uh, good girl.

Bean *grimaces at him.* **Will** *is a bit embarrassed.*

Pause.

Will   Your lip balm tastes like bubblegum.

Bean *looks like she is going to vomit.*

Will   Like, like watermelons.

I mean obviously not real ones.

Bean *ignores him.*

Will   You know just the. Like those Maoam strips.

Bean *ignores him.*

Will   Like sweets. You're [sweet] /

Bean   Fuck off.

Some time passes.

Bean *is in a daze.*

A moment.

Will *starts playing with her jars, absent mindedly.*

Will   Chilly now like, isn't it?

Bean *ignores him.*

Will   Want to play a game?

Bean *ignores him.*

Will   Doesn't have to be truth or dare.

Bean *ignores him.*

Will   Would you rather have a dick for a nose or dick fingers?

Bean *ignores him.*

Will   Bean?

Bean *ignores him.*

Will   Bean?

Bean *ignores him.*

Beat.

Will   Was just a laugh before.

Beat.

Bean *looks up properly and registers what* **Will** *is doing.*

Will   Was just a laugh before, yeh? Just a /

Bean   What are you doing?

Will *shrugs and looks confused.*

Bean   Are they my – is that.

Will   / What.

Bean   They jars?

Bean *rushes to get them,* **Will** *physically stops her, so they end up wrestling slightly.*

Bean   The fuck are you doing!

Will   Calm down /

Bean   Don't tell me to calm /

Will   You're being absolutely MENTAL /

Bean   You're being a DICK!

They untangle themselves. **Will** *holds onto the slug jar.*

Will   He's told everyone.

You do realise that, don't you?

Bean *doesn't react.*

Will   Worst shag he'd ever had.

Bean *doesn't react.*

Will   And there was me, trying to help.

Why you even tell me all that stuff, if you didn't want to, y'know?

Thought you'd be well up for it.

You're fucking weird.

Literally throwing yourself at us and then pretend you're not interested? You just go around in this floaty fucking head of yours, with absolutely no FUCKING CONCERN for anyone but YOURSELF /

You selfish fucking BITCH.

A jar is smashed. Everything slows down.

Bean *takes the slugs and starts placing them on herself.*

Will   Shit.

Fuck. Bean. Don't, I'm.

I didn't mean.

Please.

Bean, please stop.

It was an accident, I didn't mean . . .

Bean, please. It's not. It's all /

Will *goes over and tries to guide* **Bean** *up but is repulsed by the slugs.*

Bean (*screams*) GET OFF ME.

A moment.

Bean *does not laugh or react. Just stares at* **Will**.

Time passes.

Bean   What's the worst thing you've ever done?

Beat.

Will   Fucking hell, Bean.

Bean (*quietly*)   Why did you do it?

Will   It was an accident /

Bean   No.

Beat.

Will   Why did you go out with Dean?

Beat.

Bean   He asked me.

Beat.

Will   Right.

I was going to.

A moment. Let it be uncomfortable.

I'm bloody tired!

Just going to.

Nip to shower.

Will *starts to leave with a towel and miniature shampoo.*

Bean   Will.

Will *ignores her and starts to leave.*

Bean   Will /

Will   WHAT!

Bean   It's not. The shower. There – there isn't. There's not a shower block. Just. You know. A tap.

Bean *points in the opposite direction to where* **Will** *was heading.*

Bean   Outside. By the loo.

Will   Fuck's sake.

Will *leaves.*

Bean *is left covered in her slugs, her armour.*

Time passes.

Will *washes. He washes off all the dirt. Even has a fresh t-shirt. He is clean.*

Bean *puts more and more and more slugs on her.*

She rubs the dirt with her hands and puts it through her hair and on her face.

She is filthy but fearless.

Time passes.

Early morning.

They are getting ready to go home. **Bean** *is already packed and ready to go.* **Will** *is just about finished packing.*

Bean *is trying to ignore him. Just plainly waiting to go, sort of enjoying the cold sunrise and silence, making daisy chains.*

Will   Listen. Bean.

Before we go.

Got you a present.

Will *holds out his hand, grimacing, and there is a small slug.*

Bean   Oh. Thanks?

Beat.

Bean *gets up and looks at it while* **Will** *tries to slyly wipe his other hand on his jeans, disgusted.*

Bean   Um.

It's not looking too well, Will.

Will   Shit.

Beat.

Will *continues holding the slug.*

Will   Is it?

I mean. Can we. Save it?

Bean   It's just a slug, Will.

Will   Right, right. Sure. Just a slug.

Beat. Bit awkward.

Will   Just 'cause I thought you'd /

Bean   Thought I'd?

Will   Nothing! Just, you know.

Beat. **Will** *is still holding it.*

Not quite sure what to do with it now.

Bean *stares at him.*

Will   Shall I just.

Bean *continues to stare at him.*

Will   I'll just . . .

Bean *continues to stares at him.*

Will   . . . pop it back here. For you. Yeh?

Bean *shrugs and stares bemused at him.*

Will *puts the slug on the ground and wipes his hands furiously on his jeans. Maybe even gets some hand sanitiser out of the side of his rucksack.* **Bean** *watches him curiously as he does this routine.*

They both sort of stare at the slug.

Will   Ready for the big walk?

Bean   My grandad's picking me up.

Will   What? No, but we have the practice / walk.

Bean   I'm going home, Will.

Now.

Beat.

Will   Right.

Right. OK.

Beat.

Dean hasn't turned up / anyway.

Bean   Can we not?

Pause.

Will   What about the tent?

Bean   What about it?

Will   You just going to leave it?

Bean *shrugs.*

Will   Want me to show you how to take it down?

Bean *stares at* **Will**.

Bean (*challenging*)   Show me.

Will *struggles for a moment. It is embarrassing. He doesn't know how to take it down. He gives up.*

Will   I'll do that later.

I can drop it round?

Bean   It's not mine. Mr Anderson lent it us.

Will   Right.

Beat.

Will   Gonna tell me mam n'all.

About not going to Durham.

Bean   'Cause we've failed this?

Will   What? No, no, not just 'cause we've … failed.

'Cause of what I want to do.

Brighton.

Bean   Are you shitting me?

Will   Eh?

Bean   You know what, Will.

Beat.

None of this.

It doesn't.

Getting the award or not getting it.

Brighton.

It's just things.

People are more important than things.

Beat.

Will *is gutted.*

Will Your grandad'll be here / soon.

Bean Yes.

Will Course you know / that

Bean Yes.

Pause.

Bean You know. Sometimes you get glimpses of being in the right place at the right time and everything seems to align. Like. The music is right. The sunlight is right.

Will Yeh /

Bean This isn't one of those times, Will.

Bean *makes to go. Heaves on her jumper and her small rucksack.*

Will Give us a message when you / get home OK.

Bean *looks at him and ignores him.*

Will Maybe.

Next week. We could go round Stanhope?

Get some chips or something?

Go round the park and that /

Bean   No.

Beat.

Thanks.

But no, Will.

I don't think I would like to do that, actually.

A moment.

They look at each other.

Bean *leaves.*

Will *scuffs the ground with his feet.*

Picks up the daisy chain **Bean** *was making and looks at it delicately. Then destroys it and chucks it away.*

End.

For a complete listing of Bloomsbury
Methuen Drama titles, visit:
www.bloomsbury.com/drama

Follow us on Twitter and keep up to date
with our news and publications
@MethuenDrama